BUILDING FIRM

Financial Independence

with the Right Mindset

ALEX MATHERS, P.E.

Alex Mathers, P.E.

Printed in the United States of America
First Printing 2020
First Edition 2020

ISBN: 978-0-578-75280-8

10 9 8 7 6 5 4 3 2 1

For more information, contact alexmathersmindset@gmail.com

Good, better, best.

Never let it rest.

'Til your good

is better

and your better

is best.

~ Attributed to St. Jerome

DISCLAIMER

I am not a financial advisor nor an accountant. I do not have a financial certification or accreditation. Rather, I am a practicing and registered Professional Engineer (P.E.), and this book is a perspective on money, personal finance, and investing from my unique vantage point as an engineer.

The information contained herein is provided as a public service with the understanding that I, Alex Mathers, make no warranties, either expressed or implied, concerning the accuracy, completeness, reliability, or suitability of the information.

This publication contains my own opinions and is designed to provide accurate information. The reader should seek the services of qualified professionals for such advice.

ACKNOWLEDGMENTS

This book is the result of years of collaborative effort. Building FIRM is dedicated to all the friends, family, and associates who have guided me along the right path.

To my family, my resourceful wife Fran and courageous daughter Samantha, my wonderful sister Connie, my considerate mother Daryl and adventurous father Jim, thank you for your support!

Table of Contents

1. INCEPTION

The Giving Tree is a classic children's book written and illustrated by Shel Silverstein.[i] The story starts with a tree who loves a boy, who, in turn, enjoys playing with the tree, swinging from its branches and eating its apples. They have fun together, playing make-believe and hide-and-go-seek. However, as the boy ages, the relationship becomes one of the boy asking, the tree giving, and the boy taking. The boy asks for more and more, and the tree complies—eventually giving the boy almost all that she has to give.

The short story, while well received, is not without controversy. The book was banned from a public library in 1988 and receives negative reviews to this day.[ii] The story is considered by some too sad and depressing to be a kids' book. Many contend that the book is about the selfishness and narcissism of the boy, who never thanks the tree. It is said the boy is wrong for exploiting the tree's kindness. The tree never says no, and the boy seemingly takes advantage of their relationship.

These viewpoints are sympathetic of the tree's situation. Some feel pity for the tree and see the tree as a victim in the relationship. The story is judged then as one of mistreatment. These criticisms are worth considering, but there are other important points that are often overlooked.

First, when the boy in the story asks specifically for money, a house, and a boat, the tree gives him none of these things. Instead of money, the tree gives the boy apples. Instead of a house, the tree gives the boy branches. Instead of a boat, the tree gives the boy her trunk. In each case, while the tree gives supplies and support, she then leaves it up to the boy to learn how to earn his money, build his house, and make his boat.

The tree is a giving tree, as is revealed by the title of the book, but she is also a teacher. She is teaching the boy how to grow and fulfill his potential. What she gives is not what the boy asked for—but instead what he needs to make what he wants. This indirection is an important distinction, and one that is overlooked.

Just like the boy, most people want life the easy way—to be given what they need, rather than learning to make or earn it themselves. Don't take this personally; wanting to take this path of least resistance is not a trait unique to us. Mice will take the shortest route to cheese, salmon run up the slowest part of the river, and migratory birds will fly the most direct path to their nesting sites. Even physical processes like water, light and electricity take their own paths of least resistance. But, for us humans, the easiest path is not the best path for long-term growth and happiness. We need struggle to build strength, resilience and sovereignty. Hard work makes us appreciate the times of ease and prepares us for the tough times.

Taking the path of *most* resistance—the one less traveled by—will make all the difference.

For many, just like the boy, the easiest way to get what they want is to ask. If a teacher placates and gives someone exactly what they ask for, the lesson learned is dependence and reliance, instead of autonomy and responsibility. Building this "ask and you shall receive" mindset can lead to a psychological phenomenon called learned helplessness.[iii] If you train people that there is no correlation between cause and effect, they start to believe that personal success is out of their control. This backseat mentality is why life's necessities can't just be give and take. For real personal growth, lessons, skills and mindsets must be taught, learned, practiced and realized. The tree's indirect approach to the boy's personal growth into an older man avoids the pitfall of learned helplessness while not discouraging choices. She gives the boy the opportunity to struggle on his own, leaving it up to him to solve his problems.

The second overlooked point, contrasting to the sadness of the story, is the strong focus of happiness for both subjects. The tree's focus is on the boy's happiness. "Come, Boy, come and climb up my trunk and swing from my branches and eat apples and play in my shade and be happy." After each event, the author affirms "And the tree was happy . . ." Happiness, along with giving, is a core element in the story. However, these two elements are incompatible. The tree can give everything she has, except the one thing she wants to give—happiness. I believe many want to give, and be given, happiness. But, unlike apples, happiness comes from within and cannot be given. Happiness, as a state of mind and positive internal feeling of wellness, must be realized instead of received.

This juxtaposition of the tree's happiness and the reader's sadness is one reason the story is so compelling. Shel Silverstein highlights happiness as a result of personal choice and contrasting short-term suffering. The tree is happy—satisfied with her decisions to help the boy be happy—and that is what matters. I agree. Your lifelong and long-term happiness is what matters most.

The term happiness has many interpretations. The ancient Greeks had two definitions for happiness: *hedonia* and *eudaimonia.*[iv] Hedonia is short-term happiness as gratification, thrill and pleasure. Hedonia fills the desires of our senses and requires something *taken* to be happy. Eudaimonia, on the contrary, is long-term happiness from fulfillment.

Long-term happiness is lasting, self-sustaining and enduring. I define it as peace of mind by self-actualization—that is, realizing your capabilities and reaching your full potential. Eudaimonia stems from what we *give* to receive happiness in return.[v] Life, I have found, is about the never-ending pursuit of maximizing your long-term happiness. Not in-the-moment happiness, not constant happiness without any sadness or suffering, but consistent happiness resulting from fulltime fulfillment.

Next time you read *The Giving Tree* consider understanding through empathy before sympathy by identifying with the tree's choices for its own peace of mind through giving so that the boy would return. Your lifelong pursuit is defined by your personal goals. What you seek for fulfillment is up to you, but I will show you a way to maximize your long-term happiness.

Why is an Engineer Writing a Finance Book?

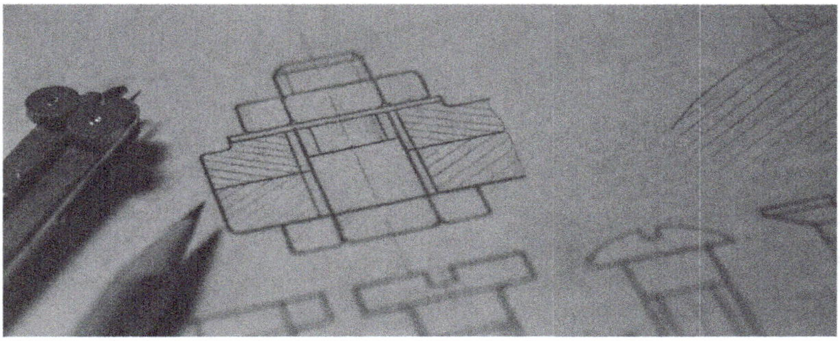

Whatever your job or occupation, personal finance is key to maximizing your happy life. I want to help you realize both *why* and *how*.

I have been working in the field of construction as a laborer, designer, engineer, contractor and owner for over 20 years. In addition, I have a master's in mechanical engineering, a handful of design patents, a state professional engineering registration, and a consulting firm. With hundreds of projects under my belt—some with budgets in the hundreds of millions—it's safe to say I enjoy and believe in designing and building things.

I am also empathetic towards people struggling with finance like myself and believe in helping others. With this book, I want to help you design and build long-term financial happiness by teaching you what I have learned is the right financial mindset. By providing illustrations, diagrams, and visual aids, I hope to teach the financial flow of money to other visual learners like myself.

Growing up with an engineering mindset, my focus was always on analytical problem solving. Luckily for me, there are never-ending problems to solve in the physical world of building, manufacturing, energy, and efficiency. At the time, I did not see a personal finance problem worth solving. It was simple—or so I thought—you work and you get paid.

But after four years of high school, four years of college, two more years of graduate school and years of working in the engineering field my frustrations regarding my personal finance caught up with me. Why, after learning and practicing advanced math, statistics, physics, statics and dynamics, do I know so little about finance? Why do I know how everything works except money?

Money, as it turns out, was one of the first problems I should have focused on. Not because it is hard—it's not—but because it is essential. Understanding finance and the value of money is key to starting life down the right path. Financial literacy is the resources, skills and understanding to make the right decisions with your monetary resources. Understanding the concepts and language of finance helps me steer my journey. Before my deep dive into the financial systems and services, I was just blindly navigating in the dark.

In the years of research—since opening my eyes to the world of personal finance and investing—I have talked to and interviewed many colleagues, coworkers, friends and relatives about money. What I have found is that I am not alone. My lack of financial education was not because I studied engineering and didn't major in finance, but because the general education system does not teach the basics of how money works, including taxes, investments, accounting, insurance, debt, liabilities and assets.

More importantly, no one learns *why* money is important. People need the financial literacy that is not part of the curriculum to plan their path forward and I want to help. Everyone also needs to understand why finance is key to long-term happiness.

Everyone has made financial mistakes, and I am no different. My mistakes came from having a misconstrued financial mindset that, looking back, could have been easily avoided. I know I am not alone. I care and I want to show you how to avoid these same mistakes, frustrations, and sources of financial unhappiness.

What Does Money Have to Do with Happiness?

Let's be clear, money can't buy happiness. Having money does not guarantee happiness. Earning money helps—but more than anything—*making* money can make you happy. Making money frees your time to pursue your purpose and find peace of mind. To be clear, making money, as I define in this book, is investing earned money from your active income to produce passive income; reaching financial independence and maximizing your long-term happiness.

Money—just like the giving tree's apples—is a tangible item. It is what we trade for value and time. Happiness, like other core feelings of fulfillment, achievement and satisfaction, is not tangible. Happiness only exists as a subjective, internal mindset.

Happiness is not only abstract but assorted. Happiness depends on the individual and their personal experiences; therefore, everyone defines and pursues "happiness" differently. Even the ancient Greek philosophers who agreed that eudaimonia is the highest good for human beings, substantially disagreed on how to define it.

Our different experiences generate different expectations. You and I derive enjoyment from completely different things. The giving tree's happiness was rooted in pleasing the boy. You may disagree with her choices and actions because they would not make you happy. You may say she is irrational. That's okay; we seek our own happiness independently by taking different paths in life. This diversity in preference is what makes the world an interesting place.

Only you know the happiness you derive from experiences. Whether you value aesthetics or function, features or simplicity, your rational is someone else's irrational. This variety in value helps make the world what it is and explains much about behavior, motivation, and markets. No one can tell you *what* makes you happy . . . only help you in *how* to pursue your happiness.

Making money can make you happy because it gives you the *time* to pursue what you enjoy in life and expect out of life. Your long-term happiness is related to your expectations of the future and feeling of fulfillment. Fulfillment starts with finding a purpose—a reason or meaning in life.[vi] That purpose is centered around giving. Fulfillment comes from accomplishing that gift.

Your expectations also affect your happiness. Past experiences mold your assumptions of the future and what you expect to happen. You knowingly and unknowingly build a vision of the future based on this conjecture. What reality brings affects your happiness. If you perform to or outperform your expectations, you are happy. If you underperform, you are disappointed. Long-term happiness is maximized by exceeding the fulfillment of your expectations during this lifelong journey.

Planning by creating realistic financial expectations and accurate value judgments—along with a milestone of financial independence—brings your subconscious hopes and dreams into a conscious reality. Making money and reaching financial independence ensures your freedom to pursue your self-sustaining happiness. Further, exceeding your expectations by maximizing the amount of money you make shortens your path to financial independence and gives you the best chance of maximizing your long-term happiness.

What is the Right Mindset?

Financial Independence with the Right Mindset (FIRM) is having the autonomy and control to make money for the time to pursue your long-term happiness.

"Life, Liberty and the Pursuit of Happiness" is a well-known phrase written by Thomas Jefferson in the United States Declaration of Independence.[vii] Jefferson may have been influenced by John Locke who, almost a century earlier, wrote in a 1681 essay titled *Concerning Human Understanding,* "The necessity of pursuing happiness is the foundation of liberty."[viii] John Locke was an English philosopher and in his essay, he observed that the pursuit of happiness is humanities foundation of individual freedom, since it gives us the ability to make decisions that are in our long-term best interest. Humans, like other animals, are excellent at making short-term decisions, but we also have the unique ability to think about the future as if it were the present. We can look ahead to financial independence, and we can take actions today which hinder us in the short-term but help us considerably in the long-term. The right mindset is about putting our future selves before our present selves, pursuing even more happiness for tomorrow.

Happiness, just like finance, is your personal responsibility and it's up to you to build happiness through your actions by focusing on what you can control. The first and most important thing you can do is take ownership of who you are and the purpose and path of your life. Only then can you start to realize your potential and find fulfillment and happiness. The pursuit of long-term happiness is about *your journey* through life on the route of your choosing, not the destination.

Whatever your background, this journey to happiness requires a constantly improving state of mind and the feeling of being in a better position than before—whether that is better knowledge, quality of life, health, experiences, or relationships.

Aristotle believed that happiness is found by pushing ourselves to find our limits and realizing our potential. In modern times, "Be All You Can Be" was the recruiting slogan of the United States Army for over twenty years starting in 1980.[ix] Corny? Sure, but true in life. We all have great capacity for learning, training, and practicing, to reach the limits of our abilities, aptitudes and skills. Your perspective on what the future can be determines your limits. If you want long-term happiness you need to reach your perceived potential. Maximizing happiness is exceeding and passing your own assumed potential.

All successful journeys require three things: freedom, autonomy and control. Freedom is flexibility, in time, opportunities and choice and comes with financial independence. Autonomy is the ability to make informed, independent, and right choices; and control is the competence to stick to these choices.

What many people get wrong about money and happiness is that they assume having money automatically guarantees happiness. While having money can provide freedom and flexibility, having money alone does not provide you with the autonomy to know where to go, or the control to stay on the right path. This is where the right mindset comes in. Having money does not facilitate your happiness, especially unearned money. You must know how to *make* money through autonomy and control; otherwise, you will *lose* money.

Realizing your present-day freedom is the first step. Even if you depend on others for financial support now, you still have the freedom to choose your path forward. The freedom to choose allows us to steer our lives exactly how we want. But with choice comes sacrifice. Making a tough choice for tomorrow sometimes means giving up something easy today.

Your route may be limited by knowledge, obstructed by obligations, or involve short-term suffering. However, gaining knowledge widens your range of opportunities, resulting in greater freedom. Obligations are overcome by using this knowledge to choose the right avenue. Short-term suffering and struggle help you recognize the right choices you have made and appreciate your long-term happiness. Financial independence provides ultimate freedom to pursue opportunities of your choosing.

Autonomy comes from understanding how your financial system works and knowing where you want to go. Knowledge of how money flows gives you the autonomy to make money and will enable you to take the path of your choosing. Knowing your path to fulfillment—and what makes you happy—guides you in making these right choices.

Finally, the right mindset and making money is all about control—control over what you earn, save, invest and grow. You can have freedom and autonomy, but if you are not disciplined you risk getting lost on your journey. Long-term happiness does not come without delayed gratification. This is not a recent development. One of the ancient Greek philosophers, Aristotle argued that true happiness is not pleasure or virtue, but the result of forgoing that short-term thrill for long-term goodwill. Hedonic happiness through pleasure is a positive—but quickly decaying experience. Happiness via delayed gratification is full-time fulfillment. Financial self-control is about staying your course with the trust you will reach your goal.

Consider an example of two B+ students from two different high schools, both with great potential. One high school is tough, has a lot of homework, tests, pop-quizzes, and flunks out many under-achievers. The other school awards easy A's to everyone. The two students graduate and are admitted to the same advanced and vigorous college program.

The student from the tough school suffered and struggled for their B+, but in doing so, has realized their potential, and gained knowledge, control, and appreciation along the way. Due to their personal growth, they have the autonomy to overcome the obstacles presented in the advanced program. The other student, entering with less knowledge and unrealized potential, is limited in discipline and is more likely to take the unproductive option of dropping out as classes get harder. Both start with the potential and freedom to succeed, but one is more likely to reach the milestone of graduation due to knowledge and control.

Financial independence is a major milestone on the right path to long-term happiness just like a graduation can be a major milestone on the road of life. It takes hard work, sacrifice, and dedication, but reaching the milestone with this right mindset allows you the freedom to explore new avenues of opportunity that come with fewer obligations. The more routes money provides you, the more choices you can make and the more freedom you will have.

While it is unknown if the student who graduated will capitalize on their success, it is more probable that they will be consistently happier than the one who didn't. With their diploma in hand and the autonomy and control gained from their experiences, they have more freedom and opportunities to pursue long-term happiness.

Personal finance is key to maximizing your long-term happiness because we trade money for time and making money makes more time. Making money requires autonomy and control. This autonomy and control help you reach financial independence which ensures your freedom (time) to pursue your long-term happiness. Maximizing the amount of money you make shortens your path to financial independence and gives you the best chance of maximizing your long-term happiness.

Who is this Book For?

No one understands personal finance by nature. It's not a skill easily learned through observation either. Personal finance is best understood through education, involvement, and practice—which involves making painful mistakes, errors, and omissions. It's very hard to bypass this educational system and come out on top. Lottery winners who come into life-changing fortunes frequently learn that having money does not mean you understand money or that you will be forever happy.

For me, it took almost 30 years to truly understand how money and personal finance work. That was not without opportunities, education, and trying. Even with degrees from a quality high school, an accredited undergraduate college and top-rated graduate program, my financial education was remedial at best. I made mistakes at every step, including relying on financial professionals who were supposed to act in my best interest.

One of my first lessons is that you cannot give away your financial responsibility. Advisor mistakes are *your* mistakes. This is not to say the financial services industry is unsound. There are many services that are worth your time and effort. But these services work best when you understand the scope and intent just as well as your consultant. You need to know how to communicate in the language of finance to be the first opinion to your advisor's second opinion.

Our financial mindset is set early in life and put into practice as we start trading our time for money. Whatever your profession, whatever your income, the earlier you understand money and how it can flow in and out of your possession the better off you will be.

I started this book as a personal finance guide for engineers and visual learners such as myself. However, I have come to find the information presented here is an ideal guide for any young student, professional, or person who wants to *see* what is typically written but not shown.

In preparing for this book, I read every personal finance book I could find. From the famous thousand-page hardcovers to the long-forgotten softbound pamphlets. All had similar messages, and all were heavily text-based. I, like many people, must read an explanation three or four times to understand it. However, if I see the description in an image, I can comprehend the message quickly.

This book is for you. My goal of this book is to fundamentally change your financial mindset with images, not just descriptions of financial terms. You will be equipped with the knowledge to make informed, independent choices, and use this knowledge to control your financial future. You will reach financial freedom and achieve Financial Independence with the Right Mindset.

FIRE and FIRM

Financial freedom is gained through independence. Financial independence and retirement are major milestones on your path to long-term happiness, but they are not the destination. A popular personal financial term is *FIRE*: Financial Independence, Retire Early. People following a FIRE lifestyle seek to reduce expenditures and increase investments in order to quickly gain financial independence with the goal of retirement at an early age.

The FIRE movement of simple living, with income from investments to achieve financial independence, originated with the early 1990s book *Your Money or Your Life,*[x] and has been refined and popularized by online blogs such as *Mr. Money Mustache* and the *Financial Samurai.*

There are no concrete rules, but generally, FIRE requires aggressive expense reduction, a high saving rate of half—or more—of your income, efficient investing, and frugal, restrictive, and minimalistic living prior to and during independence. Financial independence is defined as when one's savings reach approximately 30 times his or her yearly expenses, whereby a FIRE practitioner can quit their job and retire from any form of employment altogether.[xi]

To cover living expenses after retiring at a young age, FIRE devotees make small withdrawals from their savings, around 4% yearly. Depending on the size of the savings and desired lifestyle, it can require extreme diligence to monitor expenses and continued maintenance and reallocation of their investments.

Retirement is leaving one's income-generating full-time employment. Financial independence is the freedom to be able to retire at any time. FIRE, and specifically the financial independence aspect of FIRE, are great and worthy goals but not the end goal. Not everyone has the ambition or desire to retire early. Early retirement using the FIRE methods sometimes necessitates radical frugality and strict limits that dissuade many. Not many people realize there is a large gap between financial independence and retiring early. Sure, you can survive and be independent on a small amount of passive income, but you must first create the life you want to live before you retire. Your goal of *maximizing* happiness may require more, and you may have the ambition to work longer to reach your success target.

This is the main concern that I have with FIRE. The FIRE movement assumes your happiness is defined by frugality, efficiency, and early retirement with limitations. While this may be true, it is too presumptuous for me. I don't know what makes you happy, and neither do the believers of FIRE. Only you do.

I have used the principles outlined in this book to reach financial independence before the age of 40, and while I could retire early, I don't want to. I don't believe living with a low fixed income from this point forward maximizes my long-term happiness. I enjoy what I do for work, and I want more in life, including a better future for myself and my family.

As an alternative to FIRE, I am proposing an altered acronym: *FIRM*. FIRM stands for Financial Independence with the Right Mindset. It is having the autonomy and control to maximize the money you make for the freedom to pursue your long-term happiness. This idea keeps the financial independence milestone without exclusively pursuing an early retirement. Instead, FIRM is about continuous growth and having the right mindset to reach and exceed your happiness milestones—whatever they may be.

My goal with this book is not to tell you that you have to do one thing or another to be happy. Rather, it is to give you the tools you need to develop your own right mindset. In the end, whether your goal is FIRE or FIRM, having the right financial mindset is the key to realizing the goal of maximizing your long-term happiness.

Using the Left Side of Your Brain for the Right Mindset

Personalities in popular culture are sometimes divided into people who use the right side of their brains being more creative, thoughtful and subjective, while those who use the left side being more logical and analytical. There is no scientific evidence for brains functioning in this manner, but, if they do, I'm more left-brained.

Engineering puts science into practice as it involves the planning, designing, and manufacturing or construction of various useful items. Because of this, engineers are purpose-driven and very pragmatic. As an engineer who works in the field of construction, I am trained to think logically through strictly analytical problem solving. Everything must be organized and have an appropriate purpose and place. This book, and its structure, is no different.

I believe building a mindset is just like constructing a building. You plan, visualize, build, and then realize your goal. Therefore, the FIRM framework of this book is structured similarly to a building construction project. Starting with the goal, we move to plan and schedule, design, and finally, construct.

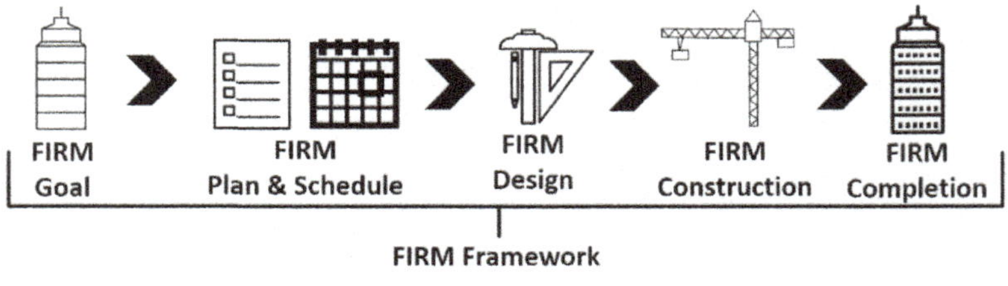

Your mindset is your method for planning, your framework for action, and your reason for doing. Planning provides a path for your journey, including milestones that define the end of one segment and the beginning of the next.

The sum of your experience, knowledge, and understanding is your framework. This is the essential supporting structure of your building. Your framework provides you with a particular set of rules to deal with problems or make decisions.

Your reason is your purpose—the why of your intentions. It defines your direction and keeps you going to reach milestones and objectives. This reason is up to you, but if we move with purpose, if we have a clear happiness goal in mind, our path is paved.

The *right mindset* is the one that keeps you on track and on the right path to maximize your happiness.

Once the building is complete, you will hopefully have learned the right mindset that is needed to help you reach financial independence and long-term happiness. Let's start building!

2. THE FIRM GOAL

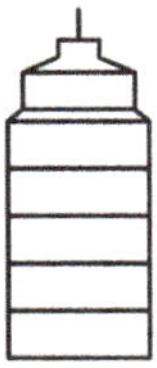

"One day Alice came to a fork in the road and saw a Cheshire cat in a tree.
'Which road do I take?' she asked.
'Where do you want to go?' was his response.
'I don't know,' Alice answered.
'Then,' said the cat, 'it doesn't matter.'"
– Lewis Carroll
Alice in Wonderland

"Where the &%@! are the electrical plans? The City Inspector will be here in less than an hour!"

Crap, I remember, thinking to myself, *I forgot to draft it.* I was late into work and when I got to my cubicle my boss was sitting at my desk looking through the various engineering drawings I had been working on that week. I had been so caught up in designing the new server room for our biggest client I completely forgot to draw up our proposed route for the new underground conduit.

We had over-promised on our construction schedule—again—and were straddling the line between making the impossible happen and complete failure, again.

"It took us weeks to get him scheduled. If we don't get sign off today, we will miss our turnover date. This is *your* job—do it or lose it!"

Making the impossible happen was not in my job description, but I had already managed to find a way every week. I looked at my watch—30 minutes. Half an hour to create something from scratch, about a subject I had no training on, to deliver to an expert I had never met, with millions of dollars and my job on the line. *No sweat, I'll get it done*!

"The plans are done," I told the boss, "I just need to print them out. Don't worry, I'll meet with him—I'm sure you've got a busy schedule today."

"Fine, just make sure we get sign off," he barked on his way out.

Ok, time to perform some magic. Quick search to find similar drawings the inspector is looking for; utility service transformer, customer side, low-voltage underground electrical conduit plans. Check. Commonly used electrical and civil engineering drawing symbols. Check. A map of our site. Check. Where we want the conduit to go. No check.

I had talked with the electrical contractor for hours the day before about everything—lighting, generator, UPS, panelboards. Everything . . . except where we wanted to route the underground electrical. There were three path options, and if the inspector didn't like the one we proposed, we would have to reschedule.

I went to our facility engineer's office to see if I could get some advice. The scene was as expected. The room smelled of a mix of sweat, smoke, and yesterday's booze. Multiple Styrofoam cups of 3-day old coffee sitting on the desk, slowly evaporating, most with a handful of half-smoked cigarettes floating on top having been extinguished in anger. It was a room the cleaning crew was strictly told not to clean for risk of throwing away an important document, folder or scribbled note. He was hunched over, yelling into the phone at the battery supplier who had dropped the load at the wrong location an hour North. His blood pressure could already be read in psi. Never mind, I thought, I'm on my own.

Back at my desk I get in the zone—deep in concentration and focusing on putting something presentable together. The sudden ring from the phone gave me a jolt. It's the receptionist telling me the inspector is here . . . and on his way over. No time to think, just put down all three, print and pray.

I give the inspector the warm and friendly greeting as required when you want someone to like you—and sign off on their obviously rushed plans. After showing him the site and boring him with as many risk-avoiding details as I can think of off the top of my head, he asks the dreaded question. "Can I see the undergrounds?"

I inhaled only a shallow breath and then struggled for another. "Sure, here they are," I said, handing him a barely passable drawing with all three options and a trembling hand.

"I thought there was just one bank of conduits. Here you have three," he frowned.

"Yes, of course, those are our three possible routes," I said, perhaps too cheerfully, trying to fake confidence.

"Which one are you going to take?" he asked.

Ok, time for a hail Mary. "Where do *you* think we should go?" I posed, knowing that this maneuver just opened up two possible outcomes that would both place me squarely in the unemployment line.

He studied the drawing in silence for what seemed like hours, tapping with his pencil on the paper. He looks at the site, back to the paper, back to the site. Finally, he looks up and says, "This way," with a smile, pointing to the shortest route.

"Funny," I said, "That's the way I wanted to go! Let me print out a new copy with that route clearly marked."

"Great, then I'll sign it off." It was music to my ears.

Impossible? Check.

Knowing Where You Want to Go

I want to show you how to pursue long-term financial happiness with the right mindset. But first, you need to answer these two questions:

Where do you want to go?

and

What do you want to do when you get there?

Where; this is not an easy question. And no, you can't ask me where I think you should go—as I did with the inspector. Life, unlike underground electrical lines, is yours. No one else can reasonably answer this question for you. I know it's easier to avoid the answer and drift through your everyday life. But if you want to pursue happiness and achieve financial independence, you need to begin by defining your dreams and purpose.

I, just like many people, grew up aimlessly thinking that the financial goal in life was all about being rich. As a kid, the idea of being rich and famous was what dreams were made of, not wealth and happiness. If asked how much I wanted to make or how much I wanted to have, my response would have been a quizzical, "Is there an answer?"

Now, I know that yes, there is. The answer becomes easier when it is understood that money is not the goal—time is. Instead of thinking about being *rich*, ask yourself what net worth would make you feel *wealthy*? Being rich and feeling wealthy are two entirely different concepts, though it can be hard to visualize the difference. When you close your eyes and picture wealth, you may see opulent people with large houses, fancy cars, and seemingly endless amounts of disposable cash. Being rich is what we see because it exists as tangible ostentatious assets.

Rich is visible worth. Rich is the tip of an iceberg; it's the small, visible part of a person's whole net worth picture. Many who seem rich are actually poor—time-poor. The phrase "money-rich time-poor" applies to those who spend time spending money.[xii] They work long hours because they have no choice to do otherwise.

Wealth is total net worth. It is the whole iceberg. But just as with a real iceberg, if you don't have a solid wealth base, the whole thing can tip over and expose a hollow underside. It is hard, if not impossible, to determine someone's total net worth because of the invisible quality of wealth.

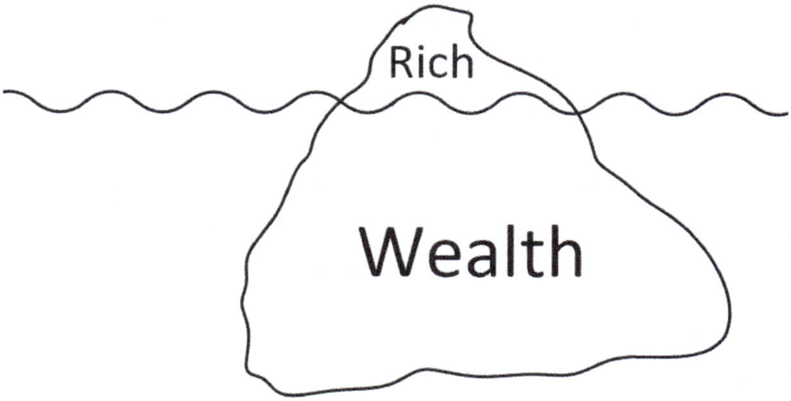

People who are only rich earn and spend; people who are wealthy make and save. Wealth is what is not seen. Wealth is the hidden—and sometimes non-existent—support structure for being rich because it is based on the intangible ability to make money by earning, saving, and investing. Wealthy people are cash-poor time-rich because their cash is invested in making money, which, in turn, makes time.

To be clear, there is nothing wrong with the rich lifestyle; but unfortunately, broadcast media, social media, and consumer marketing portray the rich as also having a high net worth and wealth. This is an incorrect conclusion. What we see as someone's riches is not equal to someone's wealth.

We fall into the trap of assuming visible riches correspond with exponentially larger wealth. However, wealth is the amount someone makes while rich is just the amount someone spends. What we see as a result is presumed to be the product of someone else's happiness, but it may not be ours. It also may be the product of short-term happiness that results in long-term frustrations. These outward projections we associate with being rich can be the opposite of wealth.

Here is what the wealthy understand that the rich do not: *Money represents time and time is the goal.* When you buy anything, you are trading your time for other people's time—money is just the medium between the two. The idea of wealth is to have enough to buy yourself the freedom to choose what do to with your time.

Do not define your dreams by the things you assume make other people happy. Feeling wealthy is about realizing your own happiness through growth. Comparing your situation to other people gives way to envy, resentment, and apathy towards financial growth. Your financial aspirations should not be based on ambiguous definitions of rich or poor. There will always be others who are richer and poorer than you. Instead, feeling wealthy should be about you reaching an ever-taller branch and looking back at your progress. Do not compare your financial position to others as the rich do. Compare your position to where you started from.

What; what would you do with your time that would make you happy? There is no right answer for everyone. Some people want to climb mountains, dive deep underwater, and jog across deserts. Some want to own antique luxury items, collectibles and rarities. Some want to build companies, run for office or help others by teaching. Most want to leave a legacy.

What is a difficult question because you have to start with the end in mind.

While you may not know what you want to do yet, Bronnie Ware might know what you don't want to do. Bronnie worked in hospice wards where she sat by the bedsides of the terminally ill for several years and was repeatedly exposed to the heartbreaking pain and anguish of dying with regret. Bronnie subsequently wrote a book, *The Top Five Regrets of the Dying*, to share her story and others. According to Bronnie Ware, the five most common regrets shared by people nearing death were:[xiii]

1. "I wish I'd had the courage to live a life true to myself, not the life others expected of me."
2. "I wish I hadn't worked so hard."
3. "I wish I'd had the courage to express my feelings."
4. "I wish I had stayed in touch with my friends."
5. "I wish that I had let myself be happier."

Of note is that none of these regrets include money; being rich or poor, but they all relate to time spent. Life is limited in time, your time. It is your choice how to spend it.

As an adult, I understand that being rich is not a goal. It is not an answer to the question. The concept of "being rich" is subjective and can mean different things to different people. When I work with my clients, my first big task is to find out what they want. Engineers design to specifications, requirements, and limits. Vague responses such as "more," "bigger," or "better" always present a challenge because they are open to interpretation. So, to be more specific, what amount of money would make you feel wealthy—feel that you have the freedom of time?

Before moving on to the next chapter, take your time and try to be as definite and sensible as possible when considering how much money you need to go where you want and do what you want. Can you do what you want with your current standard of living based on your current salary, or do you want more? Does your feeling of wealth come at $50k per year? $100k? $400k? We will do a feasibility check later, but it is important that you start somewhere.

The first step in any analytical problem-solving approach is to define what the outcome should be and set the goal. What your milestones are define how you get there. The more clearly you can define your long-term happiness, the easier it will be to choose the right path towards it. Freedom, autonomy, and control all assist your journey to long-term happiness. For you to be autonomous, you need to know your destination.

The right mindset begins with the understanding that you don't have to be *rich*, but you must have the mindset to live and feel *wealthy*. Living and feeling wealthy is not just about *earning* money but *making* money. Earning money is easily understood. You work at a job and earn a salary. But earning money is only the first step. In order to actually live and feel wealthy, you must turn your earned salary into passive income that makes you more money to further help you reach financial independence.

Hopefully, you now have an idea of how to formulate your realistic and specific milestone. Decisively figure out what makes you happy and what net worth makes you feel wealthy enough to obtain this happiness. With this milestone, it is time to formulate your paths to long-term happiness with a plan and a schedule.

3. A FIRM PLAN AND SCHEDULE

"All you need is the plan,
the road map, and the courage
to press on to your destination."
– Earl Nightingale

"Everyone, please subtract your age from 100. That number is the percentage of your portfolio that you should keep in stocks."

I looked around at the more than fifty people in the large dining room, dimly lit by the projector. *Should I even say, or do they already know*? I was easily the youngest in the room by over 30 years.

Unintentionally, I had received a mailed invitation to a retirement seminar put on by a local professional retirement planner. I knew I would probably be the only one in the room to have not heard Einstein on the radio or seen the TV show *I Love Lucy* as a rerun, but I wanted to get a glimpse of what could be my future financial situation. The meeting was at a local restaurant and came with a free dinner. My wife told me not to go—that it would be a waste of time. I figured at least I would get to try the roast duck.

"You, sir, in the back. What is your number?" *Crap, no hiding now.*

I bit my lip and tightened my fingers around the cold fork I was holding for my salad. "Sixty," I lied—sheepishly. Everyone turned and gave me a hard stare—I was younger than their kids with most of my life still ahead of me. What was I doing there they thought? I reservedly slid back in my seat.

"Wow, sixty years until you reach 100?" said the presenter in a shocked by knowingly tone. "Tell us, how much of your portfolio is in stocks?"

I tried too quickly to think of a number that would not seem outrageous towards either end. "About 50%." Another lie, but I didn't want to invite further judgment.

"Well, son, I remember my first stock, you've got plenty of time to invest, enjoy your roast duck."

Seems like I'm the one getting roasted here. I thought.

But, despite the rocky start and glaring age gap, it was a fun night. I learned a lot about what to expect (and not expect) from Social Security, annuities, and living on a fixed income.

I also realized what I wanted—to be independent of these worries. What I saw and gathered from the great people I talked to was financial fear. Fear of rising healthcare costs. Fear of an economic downturn. Fear of loss of independence. These were relatively affluent people, living in an upscale and prime retirement area. But fear was eroding their happiness.

I don't want to be afraid in the future and neither should you. With the right mindset, your path to happiness avoids obstacles such as procrastination, lack of discipline, and fear of change. Early planning for the milestone of financial independence is key because economic self-sufficiency offers the freedom to be able to retire at any time.

Without a plan and schedule, retirement can force financial independence upon you, whether you are ready or not. Building FIRM includes scheduling your financial life, planning around that schedule, and understanding how to track your milestones as time passes. Here, you'll learn how to build a financial plan and schedule to reach your financial independence.

Time and Money

Thanks to Einstein, we know that time is relative. As you get older, time seems to accelerate. You get into more set routines with fewer new experiences that change your brain patterns. This causes a time warp in your perception. Similar events make time pass quicker because your brain is not encoding new skills. This warped perception is why your younger years seem to last longer. It is why we say, "I'll have plenty of time to save later." But, while time is constantly passing at regular intervals, you don't see it that way, and this can hurt your ability to plan by helping you procrastinate.

When I was younger, I did not see time the same way I do now. Telling my younger, 20-year-old self that an investment may take five years to realize would have seemed like forever. When thinking of all the things that had happened since turning 15—learning how to drive, graduating high school, going to college—five years was an eternity. However, as an adult, five years go by in a flash. The busier we get, the easier time passes, and the more likely we are to delay doing the things we want to do.

It is important to visualize time as a constant when thinking about money. Let's take a long-range view by imagining your lifetime as a wall clock with its range of time representing your age, from 0 to 100 years old. Not everyone's life expectancy is 100, but people are living longer now more than ever and by planning for it you are ensuring both future comfort and the ability to leave a legacy.

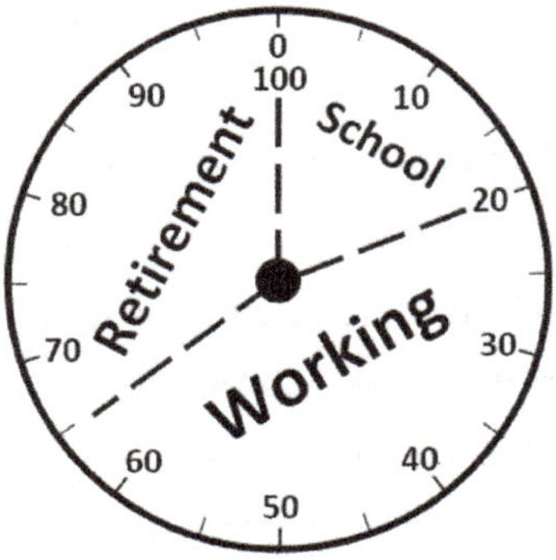

Plotting the average duration of traditional life stages on the lifetime clock shows us a more comparative picture. Because time is relative, many people have a distorted vision of how long retirement can be. Some believe retirement is only a few years. But, when looking at the lifetime clock, you can see that the time spent in retirement can be over 30 years and two-thirds of the time you spend working. Realize that for every three days you work now, you must support not only your present self for three days, but also your future retired self for two days. While you might be able to continue to work as you get older, it's not a given. Plus, will you want to?

Therefore, it is extremely important to financially prepare for retirement by planning on financial independence. Reaching this milestone earlier gives *you*, and not someone else, the autonomy to decide when you want to retire.

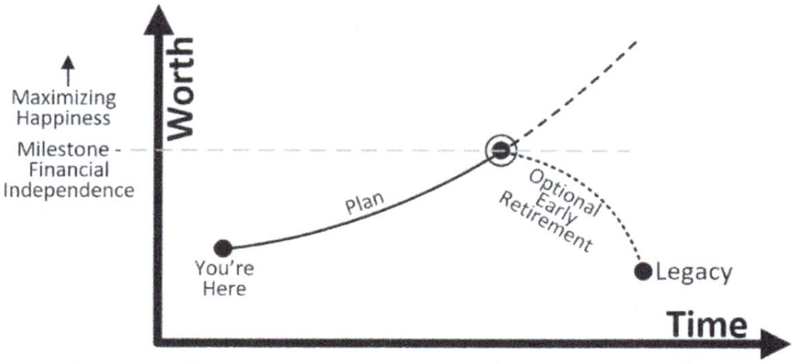

You can achieve financial independence and retire on your terms if you apply the right mindset. It's not easy because net worth is not a constant number; it is relative. The value of the money you have netted decreases over time, and the cost of what you want increases over time. Your goal of financial independence is constantly running away from you.

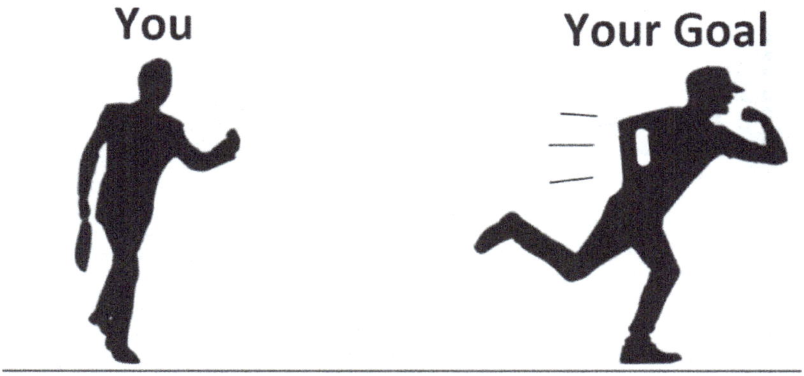

In your financial goals discussed later in this chapter, some values are given in today's dollars, and some in future dollars. This differentiation is because a dollar today is not the same as a dollar tomorrow. As noted by Benjamin Franklin, time *is* money, and just as time is relative and your perception of duration may be distorted, money is relative and distorts your perception of value. The relative value of money is defined by the time value of money.

An important fact I did not realize when I was younger: *time negatively affects the value of uninvested money.* The time value of money (TVM) means money available now is more valuable than the same amount of money in the future. Conversely, money in the past had more purchasing power than money now because of inflation and potential investment.

The fundamental financial principle of TVM holds that, provided money can grow from investments and there is inflation, any amount of money is worth more the sooner it is received. Even more critical: *as time passes, the value of money declines.* Your goal of financial independence is running away from you as you try to reach it because when it comes to money, value is variable.

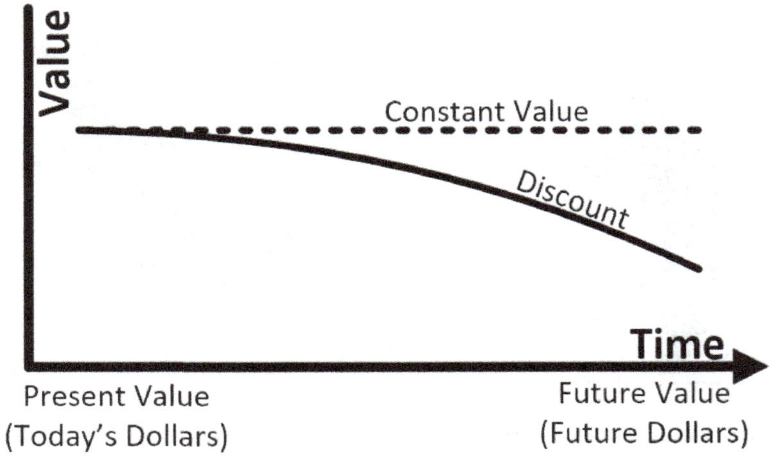

You may have heard the expression, "A dollar today is worth more than a dollar tomorrow." Money has a present value (today's dollars) and a future value (future dollars); the difference is calculated using the discount rate:

Discount = Opportunity + Inflation

The discount rate is the difference between the present value of money and its future value after inflation and opportunity. The future value of money decreases (is discounted) due to inflation and opportunity cost. *Inflation* is the increase in prices of goods and services over time (the same dollar will buy fewer goods and services year after year). *Opportunity cost* is the rate of return you would earn in an easy, safe investment instead of holding on to or spending money.

For example, would it be fair if you gave someone $100 and they return the $100 one year later? It would not. In one year, the $100 lost $3 in value (buying power) due to inflation and you also lost $3 in opportunity cost because you lost the opportunity to invest that money for a year. To be fair, they would return the original $100 and another $6 for inflation and opportunity.

This discount rate is different for everyone because inflation is variable, and it is up to you to qualify your opportunity cost. However, generally, inflation in the U.S. over the past 20 years has averaged 3% per year.[xiv] That is, 3% inflation per year, every year, for the last 20 years. In addition, an investment in the most dependable asset (deemed risk-free), a U.S. 10-year Treasury Note, returns 3% per year, every year. Therefore, every year your money is losing around 6% of its value—3% to the inflation rate plus the 3% lost opportunity cost by not investing in the Treasury Note. This 6% rate is your discount rate.

The chart below is a visual representation of the TVM.

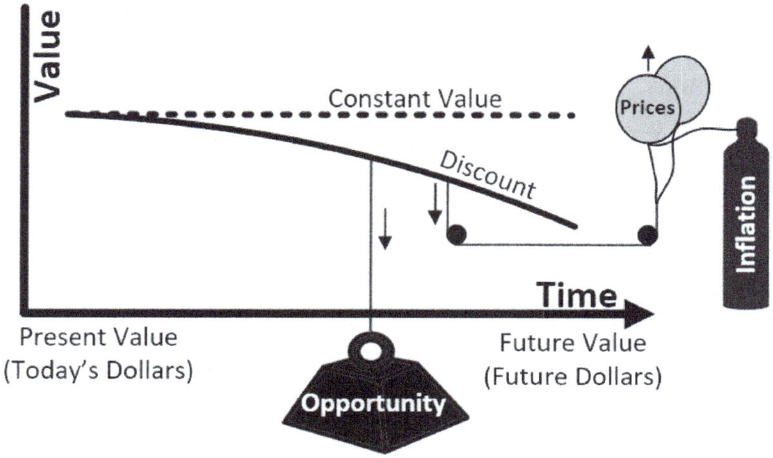

Notice that this discounted value line is curved instead of just slanted. That is because the decline in value over time is compounding. Inflation at 3% is just enough that you probably don't notice it one year after the next. Inflation erodes the value of money, slowly at first, but year after year, this erosion turns into a landslide. For example, at an inflation rate of 3%, the value of $1 is halved to $0.50 after only 24 years. If someone gave you that dollar when you were born, it would be worth only 6¢ by the time you reach 100.

How does being a millionaire sound? Great, right? My 20-year-old self would have said I was rich. Well, I am sure most of the people in the retirement dinner I attended were millionaires. The truth is if you retire at age 65 with $1 million and you decide to limit your spending to an average of $50K per year—the minimum amount necessary to cover your expenses—you will be flat broke by age 85 because of inflation. Meanwhile, you may continue to live another 15 years with increasing costs of living. Also, realize that while $50,000 may sound like enough money now, what is $50,000 going to be able to buy in 40 years' time?

Opportunity costs are even more imperceptible than inflation. We are aware of inflation because we can see the cost of a gallon of milk increase over time. Opportunity, on the other hand, is a cost that is hidden from us.

The freedom to choose allows us to shape our lives. But decisions are difficult because they also represent sacrifice. Every decision in life comes with an opportunity and a cost. Opportunity cost is what you are sacrificing when choosing one option over another. Realize that by not investing, or investing in assets that depreciate, you are missing out on risk-free money. Opportunity is a trade-off between spending your money now or investing for the future. While it does not directly reduce the value of your money like inflation, it reinforces the fact that time is money.

So how do you attain the milestone of financial independence with inflation and opportunity working against you? How do you not only keep the value of the money you have, but increase your money's value to obtain the level of worth you need to reach your milestone? To start, you need a plan.

My old boss said 'plan' is a four-letter word, referring to a set of words written with four letters which are considered profane. He was indicating that using the word plan was treated as rude and unacceptable in certain context.

Planning is important—sometimes critical—and always the right thing to do. From day-panning to financial planning our plans define our actions towards what we want; what makes us happy. But many resist or even ignore planning because of perceived pressure.

Planning allows us to work smarter, not harder. Making a plan is like using GPS to route us from Point A to Point B. Once you decide your destination or goal, you can plan appropriate steps to get there, setting intermediate milestones along the way to gauge yourself.

The right mindset includes a plan. A plan is a strategic list of steps of intended actions through which one expects to achieve a milestone. Here is a list of simple FIRM financial steps with a schedule and milestone that result in your plan:

Schedule

#1.I am __ years old, and I plan to live until age ___.

#2.I want to be financially independent by age __, which will be in the year: 20__, or in __ years.

Goal

#3.Financial independence means making $___,___ annually in today's dollars after taxes, loans, and debts.

#4.In addition, I want to leave $_,___,___in future dollars to my family for my legacy.

#5.This annual withdraw requires a total net worth of $_,___,___in future dollars.

Plan

#6.To reach financial independence by my target date, I need to invest $___,___per year and achieve a rate of return of _%.

I encourage you to take five minutes and fill in these blanks (_) above with the numbers that best describe your situation. Your financial plan is the result of how much you need to invest and the rate of return you need to achieve in order to reach your goal.

Think of this plan as your own Declaration of Financial Independence. Just as Thomas Jefferson drafted the Declaration of Independence for the North American colonies to declare themselves as independent, you should too. Draft your plan as a first step towards financial happiness.

FIRM includes understanding that you need to earn, save, invest, and compound a certain amount to make money at the rate that meets your milestone. Hopefully, you now have a realistic and specific financial goal. Again, ask yourself what will make you happy in the long-term and what net worth makes you feel wealthy enough to obtain this happiness? Alternatively, what amount would keep you from feeling financially afraid: How much would keep you from attending seminars where your age is subtracted from 100 as a gauge of your investments? Put this value in the box for #3.

You may not realize it, but you are building your autonomy. Now that you have a milestone, plan, and schedule, you need the mindset to visualize how to set up your financial flow for the future. Let's go design it!

4. DESIGNING THE FIRM BUILDING

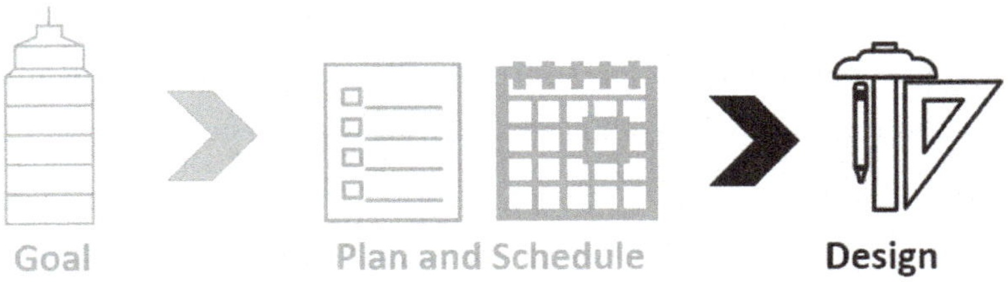

"Happiness is not something you postpone for the future; it is something you design for the present."
– Jim Rohn

It was towards the end of the day on a Friday in the summer. The clouds had parted, the sun was out, and I had plans to meet with friends at the beach after work. I had car keys in hand and checking traffic online. Every refresh made the commute 10 minutes longer. Cars were starting to pile up on the freeways and my anxiety was too. While anxiously counting down the minutes on the conveniently 5-minute fast clock on the wall I heard heavy steps down the hallway. I closed my open browser and put my keys away. I knew I wasn't going anywhere for a while. My office door opened, and my anxiety turned to uneasiness.

"Our customers don't understand why they need to upgrade their electrical service, and you need to convince them."

Here we go again. Same boss, same company, different day.

"Your engineering description doesn't work," he continued. "It's not getting through to them in the brochure."

What brochure? I thought, but didn't have to ask.

"I took your emailed description of our system, added some flair, and put it in the brochure. Here, look!"

I feared the worst as I took the glossy trifold. Sure enough, there it was:

"Our Tier 3 data center provides clean, uninterruptable power. Your power source is backed up by concurrently maintainable, N+1 generators, UPSs ATSs and switchgear allowing for any planned maintenance to take place without disrupting your operations. However, we now offer an optional, upgraded, Tier 4 level, fault-tolerant system with dual power feeds. Ask your service manager today!"

Wow, I can't believe that didn't work, I said sarcastically in my head, but without using the job-ending inflection out loud.

"How can you re-write this so we can get through to them?" the boss asked, expecting another impossible miracle.

"I can't," I said, knowing it would be frivolous.

"What!?"

"Unless they know what these terms of N+1, UPS and ATS are, there is nothing I can say to make them understand . . . but there is something I can do—I can show them."

"How?" he asked.

"I *can* take the electrical single line and make it a simple illustration showing the two separate power feeds into their equipment. No one has the time, or patience to read a thousand engineering words. But a picture is worth a thousand words and people understand pictures in seconds."

"Brilliant! Glad I gave you the idea. Draw it up and send it to marketing by the end of the day. New brochures are being printed tomorrow."

Another impossible task? Check.

Accounting – Keeping Track of Your Financial Flow

Accomplishing financial independence provides you with the freedom to explore new paths of opportunity. With financial independence, money made from your investments can sustain your expenses and debts without having to depend on a salary from an impossible employer—like the one I had to deal with as a young engineer. To reach the milestone of financial independence, you need to get into the right mindset and align your actions with your plan. This right mindset requires knowledge of the dreaded "A" word: *accounting*.

If you don't know where you are financially, you will never reach your milestone of financial independence. Having a clear understanding of the finer details of your current financial situation allows you to make quicker, better, and more confident choices. It also allows you to forecast and plan to take advantage of opportunities as they arise. Most importantly, accounting allows you to operate your personal finances like a good business, where each dollar is put to its most efficient use.

Accounting can be simple and easy, but it has a reputation for being tedious and monotonous. There are numerous applications and programs out there to help you track your finances (Mint, YNAB, EveryDollar), but no one else can do this part of the process for you; you must be your own accountant. Every dollar in your financial flow should be tracked and allocated. Never take your flow for granted. Assume that if you don't know where your money is, someone else will take it.

My issue growing up and trying to learn about personal finance was my inability to *see* how money flows. I understood some concepts, but all the finance and investing books I read were plain, monotonous text. What I couldn't see was the whole picture; how everything was related and integrated.

Personal financial accounting begins with an understanding of income, assets, liabilities, and expenses. These terms have been defined and described *ad nauseam*. But what do they look like? Well, I can tell you in a thousand words, just like every other personal finance book, and just like the company's failed brochure. Or, I can show you, using an image.

I am a visual learner and what helped me, as an engineer, was to envision personal financial accounting and money flowing like water in a system. Everyone has a financial flow system, and if you were to draw your financial flow as a series of tanks, valves, pipes, pumps, and drains, it would look something like this:

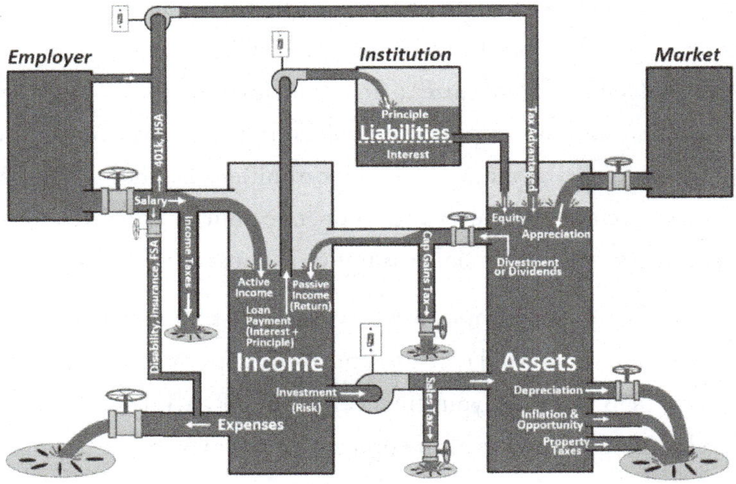

I call this your ***Financial Flow Diagram***. All this financial flow is under your control. I know the diagram looks complicated at first glance, but so can be personal finance. However, if you look at each flow independently, the system will make sense and personal financial accounting will be easier to visualize. In this chapter, I will reverse engineer this Financial Flow Diagram into its designed components, and in the next chapter, discuss how to control it.

The main design components are your three sources of money: (Employer, Institution, and Market), and your two storage locations for money: (Income and Assets). Let's break the Financial Flow Diagram down and take a closer look at income and assets and how to account for them.

Income – The Tank of Your Bank

You give your employer your time and effort, and in return, you get paid. This pay may be a wage, stipend, and/or gratuity. For simplicity, I will lump these together as a *salary*. That salary is the active income part of your personal revenue. As explained in a later chapter, you have control over the amount of income you earn. In this image, salary from work is represented by the water (money) flowing into your Income Tank.

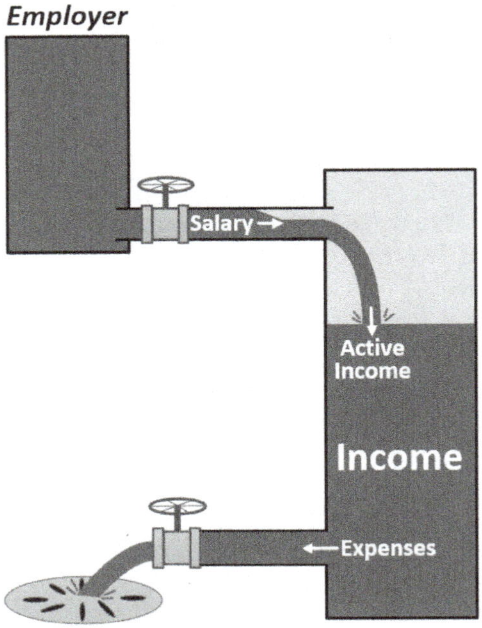

The control you have is represented by the valve in line with the salary flow. As you work over time and hopefully increase your salary, you open the valve and increase the amount of money flowing into your Income Tank. Think of your Income Tank as your bank account. Its level is defined by how much cash you keep on hand and in a bank.

At the same time, you have expenses. These expenses drain money out of your Income Tank. Expenses include rent, gas, food, household items, clothes, entertainment, and other items you buy that have no resale value. Just like the money flowing through the Salary Valve, you also control the amount of money flowing out of your Income Tank through the Expenses Valve. If you pay a lot of rent, you are opening the valve and allowing more of your salary to flow out and down the drain.

The level of money in your Income Tank is defined by income minus expenses, which can be a reflection of your spending habits. The larger your salary, and the fewer expenses you have, the higher your Income Tank level can be. If you have more expenses flowing out than salary flowing in, your Income Tank will drain until it is empty.

The following may seem like a basic concept, but I want to stress it here: *You must produce more than you consume.* Your independence and autonomy are based on the amount you produce (earn) minus the amount you consume (spend). Your happiness is maximized by giving more than receiving. When you think with a producer mindset rather than a consumer mindset, you are working with the right mindset.

Assets – The Tank with the Swank

Now, not all your money is contained indefinitely in your Income Tank. Some purchases are expenses and sometimes you buy items that have resale value. These are *assets.* Cars, houses, electronics, collectibles, stocks, and bonds are all investments that will fill up your Assets Tank. To visualize this money flow, I add a pump with a switch and second tank, your Assets Tank, to your Financial Flow Diagram:

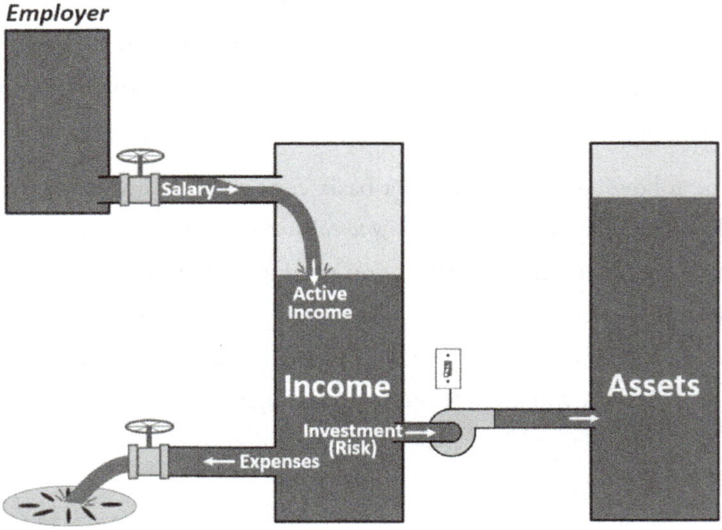

Because you control when you buy assets, you have control over the pump that moves money from your Income Tank to your Assets Tank. This control is represented by the switch connected to the pump. When you make a purchase or acquisition of something that has resale value, you are intentionally moving money from your Income Tank into your Assets Tank. This act of buying, purchasing, or acquiring an asset is an *investment.*

While it may seem like your assets keep their value, over the long run, they may not. Your assets' value can *appreciate* or *depreciate* over time. You give the market your risk by holding these assets, and hopefully, in return, your assets gain value (appreciate) over time. However, assets can also lose value (depreciate). This not easily predictable change in value is the risk you take whenever you invest—and is represented by water pouring into and draining out of your Assets Tank.

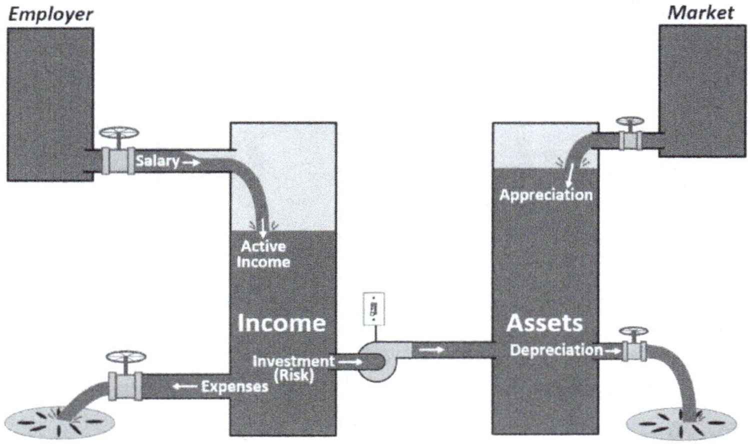

I have placed control valves on the Appreciation inlet and Depreciation outlet, as you do have some control over this change in value. While you cannot fully control the appreciation and depreciation of individual items, you can control what types of assets you buy; therefore, you can control your overall level of worth in your Assets Tank.

Further control comes from your ability to regulate the amount of money you *make*. As your investment assets appreciate, you may choose to sell or divest to get a return on that investment. With some investments, you don't even have to sell to get a return. Regular dividends, interest, and income can be gained from some forms of assets. This is where the second flow of money—passive income—can enter your Income Tank. As previously stated, the right mindset begins with the understanding that living wealthy and long-term happiness is not about *earning* money but *making* money.

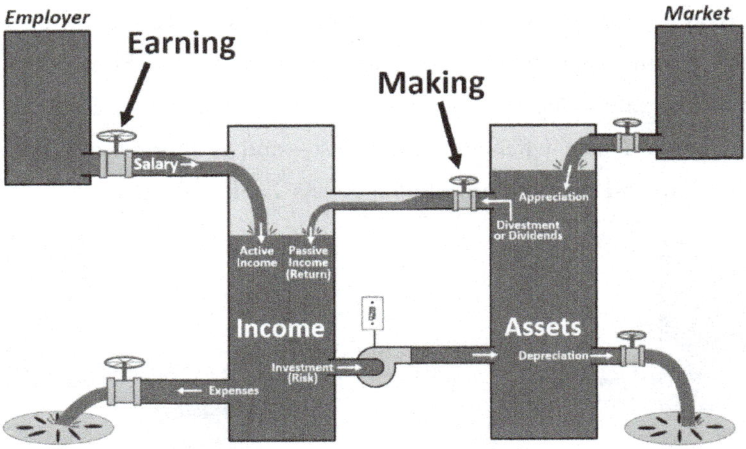

Here is where you can visualize the difference. You *earn* money from your employer. This is your primary source of money and your active income. *Active income* is the money you receive for doing your regular 9-5 job, where you are directly compensated for the hours you work. You give time and you get money. Simple.

Conversely, you *make* money from your assets via the market. *Passive income* comes from investments and is not directly tied to time. Passive income is money that you consistently make, whether you spend your time on it or not. Passive income is not a second job; rather, it is money you make from the divestment (selling) of an asset, being paid dividends or interest, or collecting from an income-producing asset such as rental income.

While you have some control over the money you earn, you have full control over the money you make. Unlike your salary, which is at someone else's discretion, you have full authority over your assets to determine when, what, and how much you want to divest.

Having the right mindset is realizing this difference between earning and making. Making money comes from the right combination of earning, saving and investing. Making money means you have control over your personal finances. Maximizing the money you make maximizes your freedom and allows you the opportunity to pursue your long-term happiness.

Financial independence is when you make more money than you spend. It is when you don't have to depend on earning income from an employer. That is true wealth and the financial independence milestone: the freedom to be able to retire at any time.

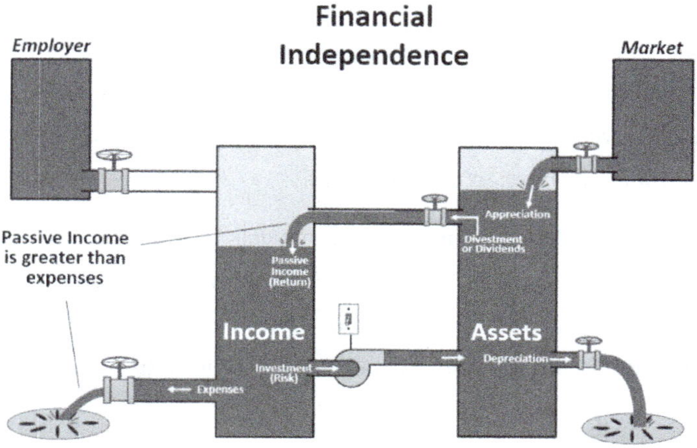

Debt – Liabilities in Life

Debt is all about trust. Lending is based on the trust that someone in debt to you will pay you back with interest. Engineers like myself are risk-averse and mostly will avoid debt at all costs. We fear debt because we fear the unknown. We have been taught that debt is bad. However, debt can be good; and credit, which is your ability to take on debt, is a necessary tool for building wealth.

Your ability to borrow is contingent on your credit scores. A credit score is a numerical expression that represents the creditworthiness of an individual. A credit score is primarily based on a credit report typically sourced from credit bureaus on past debts.

Here is how debt fits into your Financial Flow Diagram. Let's say you are earning money, but also spending money at a rate where you don't have enough extra money saved in your Income Tank to purchase a large ticket item like a house, a car, an education, or some consumer items.

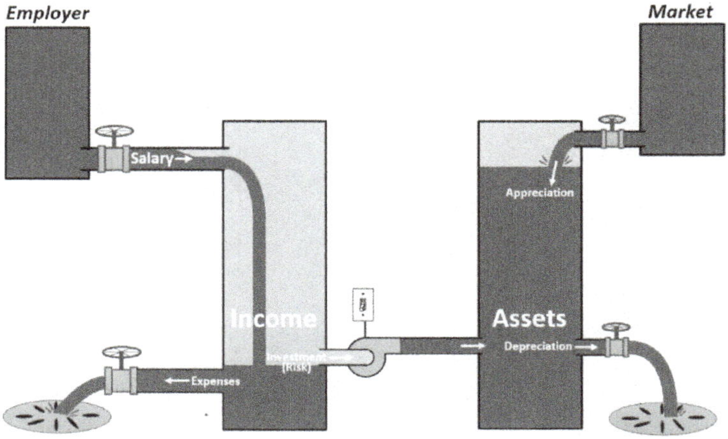

You need more money to purchase an item and you need the money faster than you can fill the tank with your income. Consequently, you go to a financial institution (typically a bank) and you ask to borrow money. This is a loan, also known as consumer credit. This loan can be an unsecured loan, such as a credit card or student loan, or a secured loan, such as a mortgage or car loan.

With secured loans, the debt is protected by collateral and because of this the interest rates are usually lower. This collateral is the asset being purchased. Unsecured loans do not have collateral and therefore have higher interest rates. For example, student loans are unsecured term loans, meaning you have a certain amount of time (term) to pay back a fixed amount of money. Credit cards, on the other hand, are unsecured revolving loans. This means that you can continue to accrue debt on the account as you're paying it off and there is no set end date. Secured loans typically have lower interest rates than unsecured loans.

With secured loans, you are not directly borrowing money to pay for an item. Instead, the institution purchases the asset in your name. They give you full rights to use that asset, but not ownership, and in return, you pay them back the cost of the asset plus interest over time. The amount or rate of this interest is either fixed (known) or variable, a.k.a. adjustable (unknown). Interest rate is the amount charged, expressed as a percentage of principal, on an annual basis. This rate is expressed as the annual percentage rate (APR).

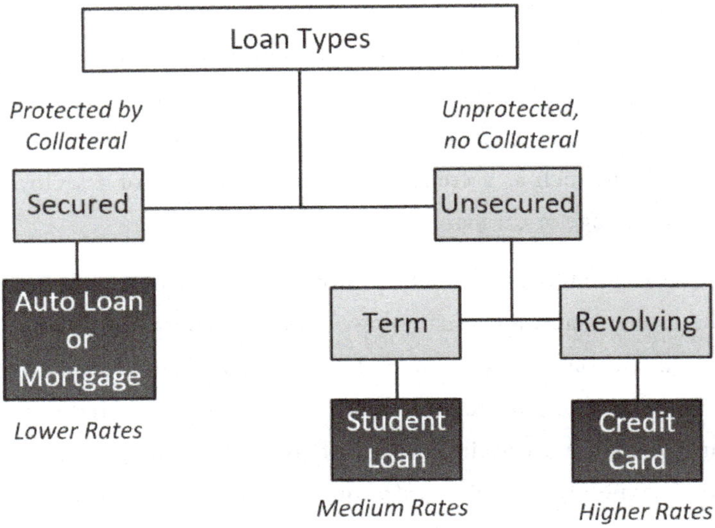

The total amount of the principle plus the interest are your liabilities. To represent this component of the money flow system, I created a liabilities tank.

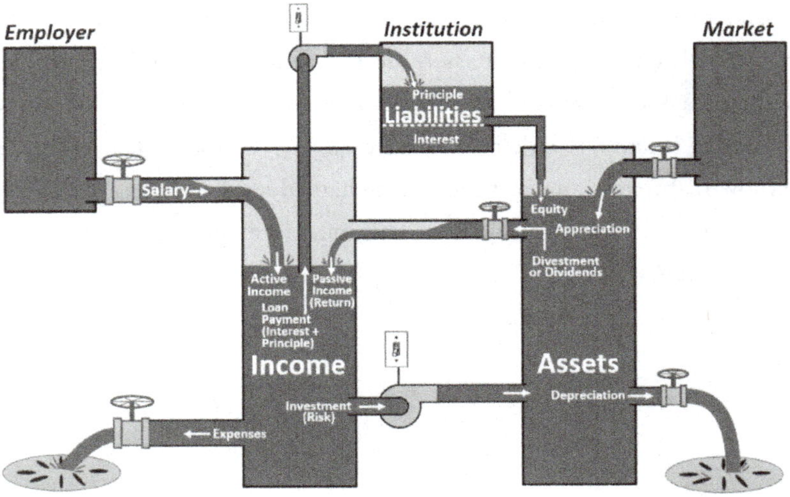

As you pay back the institution, you are paying a sum that includes both the principal and interest. The good news is that as you pay off the principal, you gain partial ownership of the asset that is equal to the amount of the principal paid. In this way, the principal you pay the institution passes through their tank and into your assets tank. After paying off the full amount of the liability, you gain total ownership of the asset. You keep the principal, and the institution keeps the interest.

The principal you keep in an asset is called *equity*. Equity is one's amount of ownership in any asset after subtracting all debts associated with that asset. Debt is the remaining amount of principal and interest associated with an asset's loan. As you start paying off a loan, you have little equity and mostly debt remaining. But, through monthly payments over time, you increase your equity and reduce your debt in the asset.

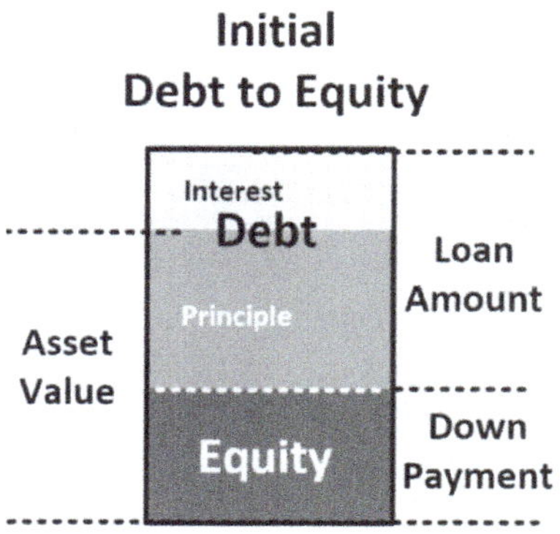

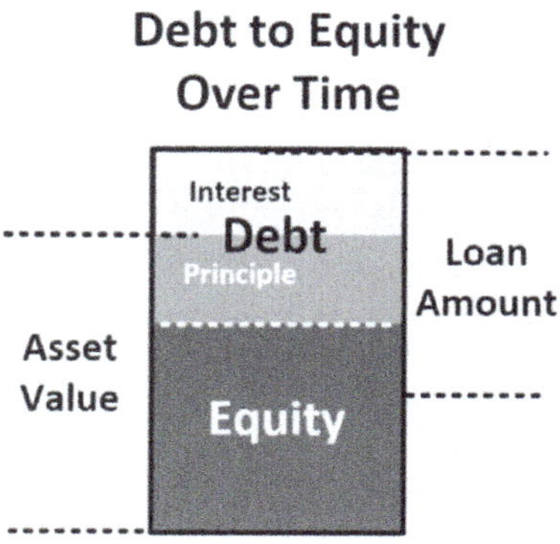

However, it is important to know that while principal is a fixed amount, *equity is variable because it is tied to the value of the asset.* If you buy an asset (such as a car) with a bank loan and the asset's value depreciates, your equity decreases along with it. But your loan amount stays constant. The bank does not care that your car's value has decreased. They still want the principal and interest you owe them.

Let's compare this to an asset that may appreciate, such as a house. If the house's value appreciates over time, your equity rises along with it. Same with the car loan, the house loan (mortgage) amount stays constant, but your equity increases in proportion to the asset appreciation.

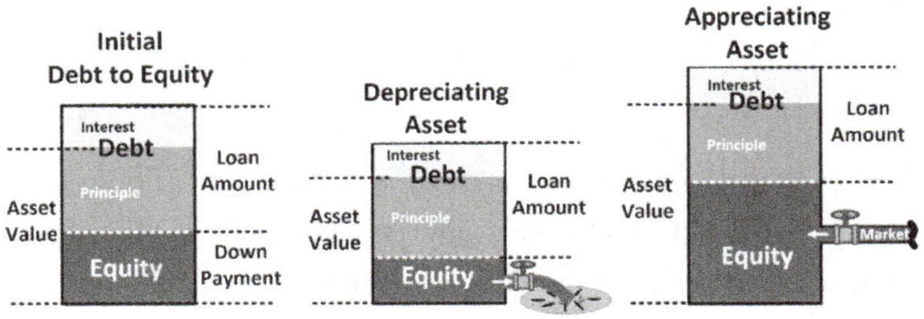

(Example: A Car) (Example: A House)

The right mindset includes the understanding that debt is tied to a loan amount and equity is tied to an asset's value, but an asset's value is not tied to the loan amount. This means that while an asset's value can change, the loan amount will remain the same. Debt can be good because you have the opportunity to leverage other people's money to make an investment. Good debt is a low interest loan used to buy an appreciating asset. Bad debt is high interest loans used for depreciating assets.

Taxes

Taxes are most likely your single biggest lifetime expense, and therefore, necessitate their own flows. They are the fee for living in a city, state, county or county. Taxes highly impact your financial picture because any dollar you earn could end up being taxed twice or even three times: once when you get paid, again when you invest in an asset, and a third time while continuing to own that asset or when you sell it.

While taxes are unavoidable, they can be managed and limited. You've probably heard that death and taxes are the only certainties in life. This is true, but another axiom should be, "Proper tax management is the only certainty to making wealth in life." It's slightly less catchy, but still true.

Some understand debt and taxes and use them to their advantage. Others pay more tax than they need to because of the daunting task of understanding tax liabilities. The tax code is certainly not a glamorous topic. To help guide you, I will break down the different taxes and help you understand where and when they are collected. There are four major types of taxes: income, property, sales, and capital gains taxes.

First, let's look at income taxes, as they are the first and largest taxes you will see. As a standard W-2 employee, taxes are taken out—or withheld—as soon as you are paid by your employer. Also, they are progressive, meaning that the tax rate increases as the taxable amount (your income) increases. The average U.S. citizen's effective tax rate, including federal and state income tax, is 25-30%,[xv] which reduces your salary by one-quarter to one-third right off the top. What's left is your net income.

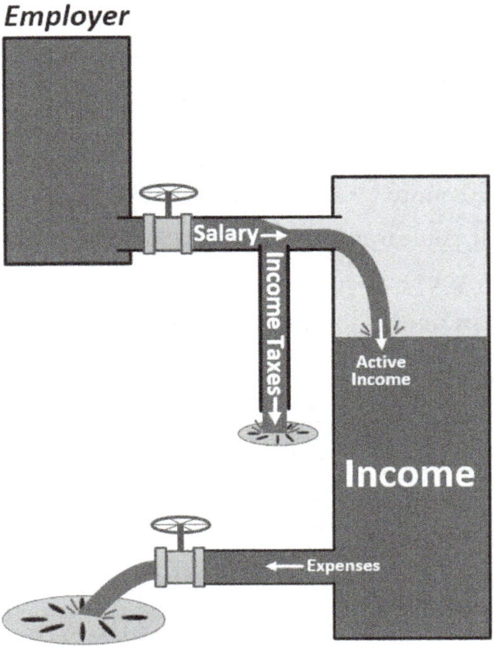

In the U.S. federal withholding taxes take the largest percentage of your income. A taxpayer's average tax rate—or effective tax rate—is less than their marginal tax rate (their tax bracket).

Included in income taxes are Federal Insurance Contributions Act (FICA) taxes. FICA is the federal law that requires you to pay three separate taxes from your salary: Social Security tax, Medicare tax, and state withholding tax. The first two are flat taxes as opposed to progressive taxes. This means that everyone pays the same amount; it doesn't change based on your salary. However, the state withholding tax is a progressive tax, and this tax rate varies wildly from state to state. Again, there is no control valve on your income taxes drain line. Therefore, it is important to understand how to indirectly regulate your active income to limit your losses to income tax. This is explained in future chapters.

Property taxes are the second type of taxes. They are a state tax that comes out of your assets tank. Property taxes typically are for real estate, but some states also tax cars and boats. Property taxes are unavoidable, but they also can be managed. It's important to understand what your state includes in property taxes, how your state calculates property taxes, and how often your property's value is reassessed to determine the tax amount. This tax can greatly affect your realized property value over time.

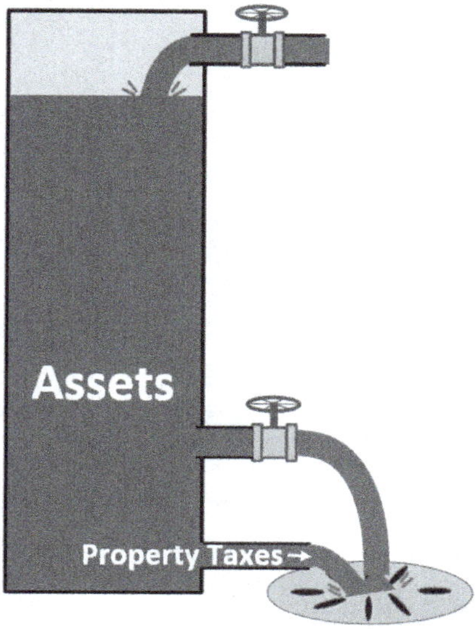

The third type of taxes are sales taxes. When you make a purchase and transfer money from income to assets, depending on the type of asset, you may pay sales tax. These sales taxes can be state and local taxes, specific goods taxes, known as excise taxes, and use tax. Excise taxes, such as a gas or cigarette tax, work differently than sales taxes and are focused on specific items considered superfluous or unnecessary goods and services. Use tax targets purchases made outside of a given tax jurisdiction, for example, in online sales. Excise tax and use tax are similar enough to sales tax regarding your finances that I am grouping them all together.

A sales tax is a tax paid to a governing body for the sale of certain goods and services. Laws allow or require a seller to collect tax funds from a consumer at the point of purchase. Sales tax is levied at the point of sale, collected by the retailer, and passed on to the government.

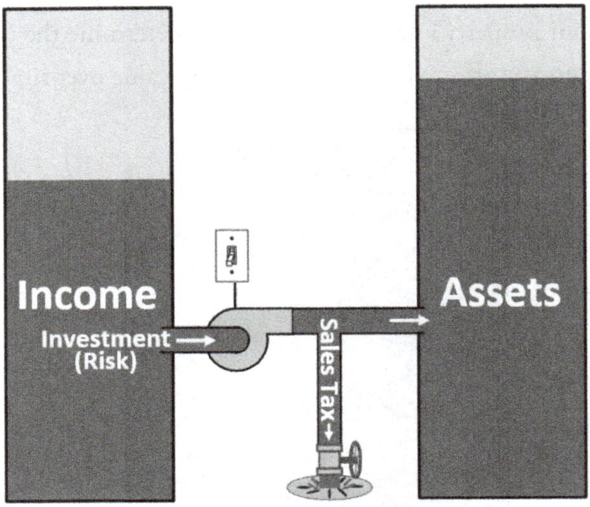

Not every asset purchase requires you to pay a sales tax, which is why there is a control valve in line with the drain. You control what types of assets you purchase, and therefore you have some control over the amount of sales tax you will pay. That's why it's important to understand the type of asset you are purchasing and the tax implications. When buying a car, you, as the buyer, must pay the sales tax. When you buy a house, however, typically the seller pays the sales tax (in this case, it's called a transfer tax). If you buy a stock or bond, no one pays sales tax.

The final type of tax is capital gains. When you sell an asset that has appreciated in value for a gain, you must pay a capital gains tax. Did I mention you could be taxed three times? Let's say you buy an antique vase. First, you paid for that with your taxed income. Second, you paid sales tax at the time of purchase. Then, let's say you find out the vase was once owned by the emperor of China in the 14th century, so you take it to an auction to sell it for a profit. Now you must pay a third tax—capital gains tax.

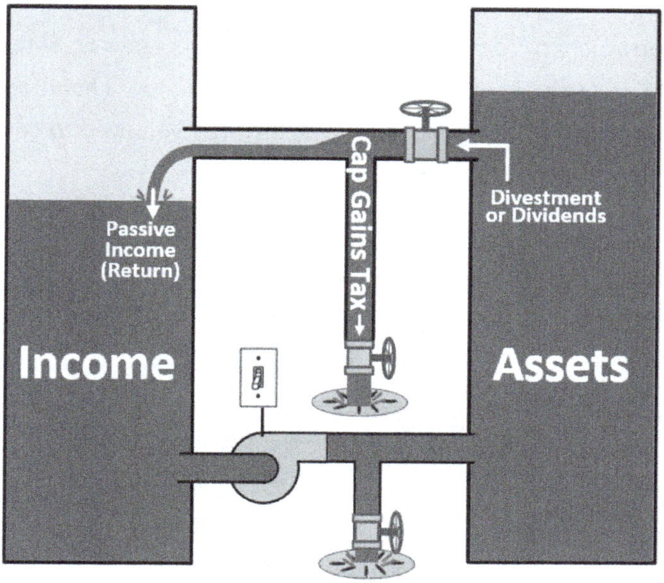

Capital gains are the profits realized on the sale of assets that are greater than the purchase amount. The most common capital gains occur from the sale of stocks, bonds, precious metals, and property.

The capital gains tax also has a valve on it because it is one of the tax rates that you can control. What you sell and when, and even what you buy, can control the rate at which you will be taxed. For example, capital gains taxes from stocks can be either long-term or short-term. If you sell a stock less than a year after you bought it, you will be charged a short-term capital gains tax rate, which is equal to your income tax rate. However, if you hold a stock for more than a year before selling it, you will be charged at a greatly reduced long-term capital gains tax rate.

Discount Drains and Pre-Tax Deductions

Completing the design are drains on assets and income resulting from the discount rate and optional pre-tax deductions. The inflation rate and opportunity cost drain your income and assets tanks at a steady rate, as already discussed in the Plan and Schedule chapter. These factors will drain your net worth year after year, which is why you need to continually increase your income and appreciation.

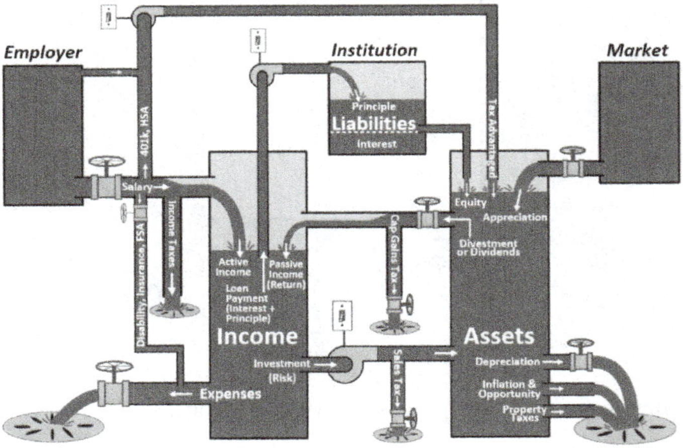

Pre-tax deductions come from your employer's savings programs. These include retirement plans such as a "401(k)" and a Healthcare Savings Account (HSA), as well as health and life insurance and a Flexible Spending Account (FSA). 401(k)s and HSAs can include matching contributions from your employer and are taken out of your income stream before income tax is calculated. And once taken out, that money will sit in investment accounts that are also not taxed.

Health and life insurance and FSAs are also pre-tax funds removed from your income flow and are used to directly offset expenses. When you bypass the income tax drain by funneling money to these options, it's possible to save a significant amount of money.

Classifying Your House or Home

There's much disagreement in the personal finance and investing world about how to classify your residence, if you own one. If you own your home or ever consider buying one it is important to understand if it is an asset or a liability; an investment or a money pit. Most importantly, should the value of your house be counted toward your total net worth for your milestone of financial independence with the right mindset?

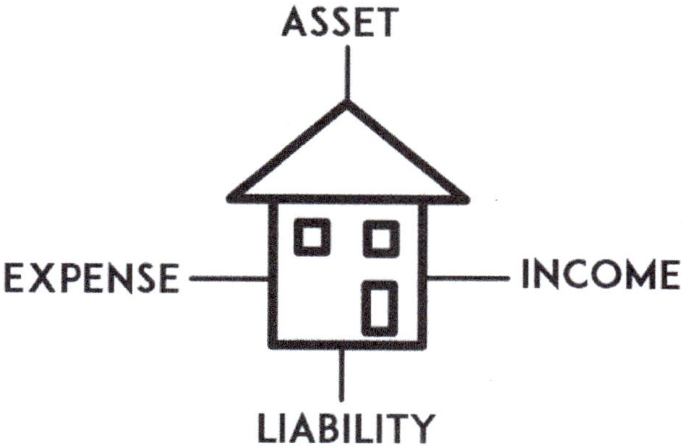

Let's start with this: Your house is two things. First, it exists on permanent land, lasting or intended to last indefinitely. This land is a very real, fixed place in space. It cannot be moved. It cannot be destroyed. It is defined by boundaries relative to neighboring space. This space is a finite resource.

And second, your house is also a structure or a shelter within this area. It is a tangible, physical, long-term resource. Shelter, along with air, food, and water, are among humans' basic needs to survive and thrive.

Some say your house is an asset because it is your property. Others say it is a liability because of the risks involved. It may be an expense because every month it takes money from your pocket. Your house could also produce income as a rental, farm, or workplace.

To be clear, I am talking about owned, private real estate that serves as your primary residence. Owning real estate is a major investment class all on its own. When investing in real estate, there is an important distinction between real estate you own for the purposes of renting out and real estate you live in and use yourself. A primary residence is property that you live in for the majority of the year whereas an investment property is one that you own but trade the right of full access to a tenant in exchange for rent.

Real estate is an asset. More specifically, the space it occupies is a fixed asset in that it is a long-term, unconsumable resource. Investment properties are assets; there's no debate on that. So, what is it about your house that makes this a confusing and contentious subject?

The first cause for confusion is how some people define assets and liabilities. Remember, an asset is anything that has resale value. Just because you may sell an asset for less than you bought it does not change what it is.

A liability is a responsibility. It is an obligation. When you own real estate, you are responsible for a lot of things: property taxes, insurance, utilities, the well-being of its occupants, taking out the trash, and only slightly more importantly, your mortgage. Your house is an asset that carries a lot of liabilities. The loan on your house is its primary liability.

The second cause for confusion is how your house starts as an asset to someone else and becomes your asset over time. With the typical 20% down payment for a home loan, you only own (or have equity in) 20% of the house on your closing date. The mortgage-lending bank owns the other 80% of "your" house. If you buy a million-dollar house with 20% down, are you a millionaire? No, you have only reserved the right to a million-dollar asset, provided you make all the remaining necessary payments.

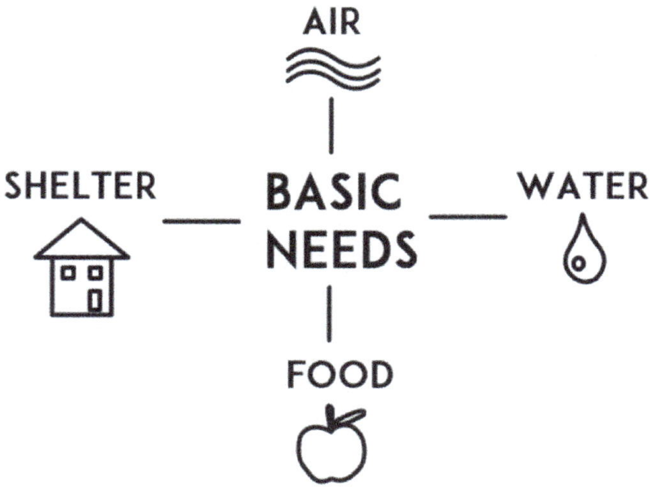

The third confusing idea about your house is its purpose. There are lifelong expenses related to your basic needs. Air is free (at the time of this writing), but water, food, and shelter all are required expenses.

Your primary residence is an expense. You cannot escape this expense, but you can reduce it. Rent will always increase. Buying and owning a house can save you some of this living expense over the long run because you are locking in the cost of a shelter.

So, what is your house? I believe it is an *asset*, but not an *investment*. It is a special type of asset that I will call a 'fixed expense asset', which means it should be viewed and treated as a lifestyle expense.

Your house, like stocks, bonds, and cars, is an asset. But unlike stocks, you can't sell your house freely. Unlike bonds, your house does the opposite of pay you dividends. It is a money pit. The bigger the house, the bigger the pit. Houses have expenses called *carrying costs*: the cost of insurance, taxes, depreciation, the cost of capital, and opportunity costs. Any level of lifestyle luxury you prefer over your basic shelter needs is an added expense.

Also, unlike a car, shelter is a basic need, and often a predominant expense. This means that if your primary property appreciates in value, that's great, but you can't access that added value without selling your house and moving. When you sell and move, you take the equity with you to invest in the new house.

In general, home values rise and fall together. If you want to buy a comparable house in the same area as the house you're selling, it likely will have risen in similar value, reducing any gains. Appreciated equity in your house is frozen. You can borrow some of the appraised value of your home through a HELOC (Home Equity Line of Credit), but free and clear equity can't be realized unless you sell for a profit and buy a less expensive house to realize your equity gains.

Your house is an expense asset because it is one thing you can buy that addresses a lifelong expense. When calculating your total net worth toward financial independence, the value of your house should not be added unless you are also subtracting the cost of an acceptable alternative shelter for the rest of your lifetime. A typical valuation of a primary residence to conform to what is typically represented on a Net Worth statement—the fair market value is listed as an asset and the mortgage balance is listed as a liability.

So, what are people saying when they say your house is not an asset? They are saying it's not a great one. Ownership of a house can result in a financial gain, but not without risk and significant opportunity cost. There are other investment assets with much better risk-return profiles than your house. When buying a house to live in with the right mindset, understand the opportunity and consider the costs.

Total Net Worth

Your milestone is financial independence, which you defined in the Plan and Schedule chapter as a total net worth of $__,___,___in future dollars. Your total net worth is the content of your Assets Tank minus your Liabilities Tank.

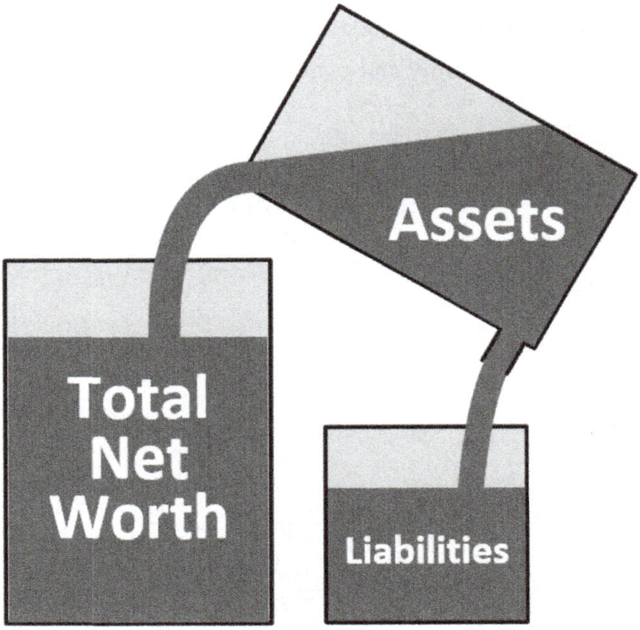

Notice that your salary and your Income Tank are not included in your total net worth. This is an important distinction between being rich and living wealthy. Wealth comes from assets and is included in your total net worth. If you hold onto your salary through saving and investing in assets, you will gain wealth and have a higher net worth. If you spend your salary on expenses, it does not count toward your total net worth. It is as if the money was never there.

Milestone Reached

Congratulations! You have completed the design of the Financial Flow Diagram and now know how to visualize it. You now have a blueprint to the right mindset and your financial autonomy. You know the theory; to maximize your long-term happiness, you need to maximize the money you make by earning, saving, borrowing and investing.

The hard work is over and it's (mostly) downhill from here. Now comes the fun part. Let's put the theory into practice. Let's start constructing your right mindset and learn the control to follow the right path to your financial independence and long-term happiness.

5. CONSTRUCTING THE FIRM BUILDING

"It is not the beauty of a building you should look at;
it's the construction of the foundation that will stand the test of time."
— David Allen Coe

"I guarantee at least two people will be fired by the end of this," said my coworker in their usual conspiracy theory tone.

But unlike the one about the higher-up spying on us, or the employee who was secretly trying to tank their project to prove a point, I believed this theory . . . even though the project hadn't even kicked off yet.

It had been several years since I had been performing the impossible with my previous company. I was now in a high-profile engineering role in a large Fortune 500 company and I was trying to work my way up. I got lucky when the Board approved a brand-new building, and I was appointed lead engineer.

With the accelerated and aggressive schedule promised, the amount of money being budgeted, and the usual politics, there was certain to be winners and scapegoats in the high-stakes game of marquee project construction.

"Yeah, one of them is probably going to be you," I deadpanned back to them.

"Good, I can use the severance!" We both chuckled.

We were going headfirst into a two-year, multi-building, overtime-inducing construction project with all the superlatives: biggest, boldest, best. The design was complete; now it was time to put the rubber to the road.

What I like about construction is that there is nowhere to hide. During design, there are estimations, calculations, promises and pitches, that all add up to trust. When construction is over, either you were right, or you were clearly wrong.

Like any industry, the field of construction involves both theory and practice. Engineers like myself design to theory; contractors implement based on practice. You have your milestone, plan, schedule and Financial Flow Diagram design. Now it is time to execute, build the mindset, and put it into practice.

What I didn't know growing up is how money flows and how to control my flow. In the previous chapter, we reviewed the Financial Flow Diagram and its components. In this chapter, we will construct the right mindset building floor by floor. I discuss the five floors of building your worth through a right mindset to control your financial flow and reach financial independence.

The floors I will cover include:

1. Earning
2. Saving
3. Borrowing
4. Investing
5. Making

Each of these floors requires making choices for better control over the outcome. I will show you how to make informed choices that will help lead you to your milestone of financial independence.

The First Floor: Yearn to Earn

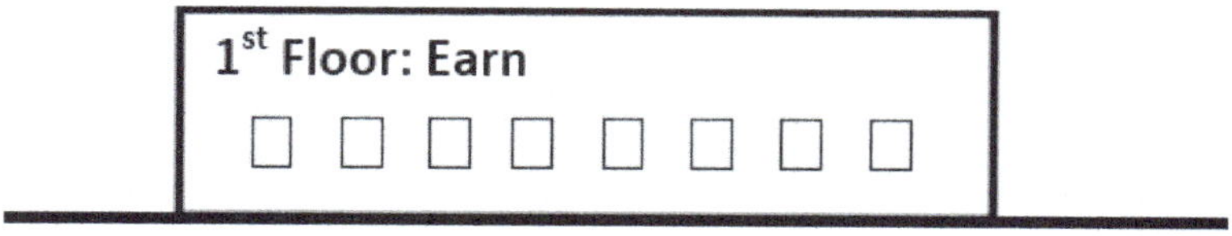

"They've already started pouring the first-floor concrete!" my coworker exclaimed a few weeks into the project. "We haven't finished submittals yet; the anchors could be in the wrong place!"

"Better update our resumes," I joked. But in the back of my mind, I knew it could be an issue. If the anchors aren't set right, they will have to come back and drill, which costs ten times more.

"That's what we get with the accelerated schedule, no time to do it right," they said as a matter of fact. "How can we confirm the anchor locations without knowing the final equipment mounting requirements?"

"We can't," I said.

"So, what are we going to do?"

"Nothing, it is out of our control," I advised. "Don't worry about things you can't control, like the anchor locations. Let the project manager worry about that. We will focus on what we *can* control, like getting the submittals reviewed as fast as possible. If we miss the pour dates, so be it."

"Ok, but if the project manager calls us out in the meetings . . ."

I interrupted them, "Then we will deal with it."

With personal finance, just as I told my coworker, focus on what you can control. The primary flow into your Income Tank is the money that you earn. Controlling this flow is critical to increasing your total net worth. A large portion of this book is dedicated to generating passive income, as it is the more hidden of the two incomes. However, that is not to say that your active income is not important. The valve that is connected to your employer is your Earning valve.

You have control over this flow. To reach financial independence sooner, you need to maximize this stream of income by opening this valve as much as possible. No matter what your occupation, your salary depends on three key amounts: the amount of value you provide to other people, the number of people that you provide value to, and the amount you negotiate for that value. For example, a lawyer provides a lot of value to a limited number of people but can negotiate a high rate due to their limited competition. A restaurant dishwasher—as I was in college—provides not much value to a small number of people and has little room to negotiation with so much competition.

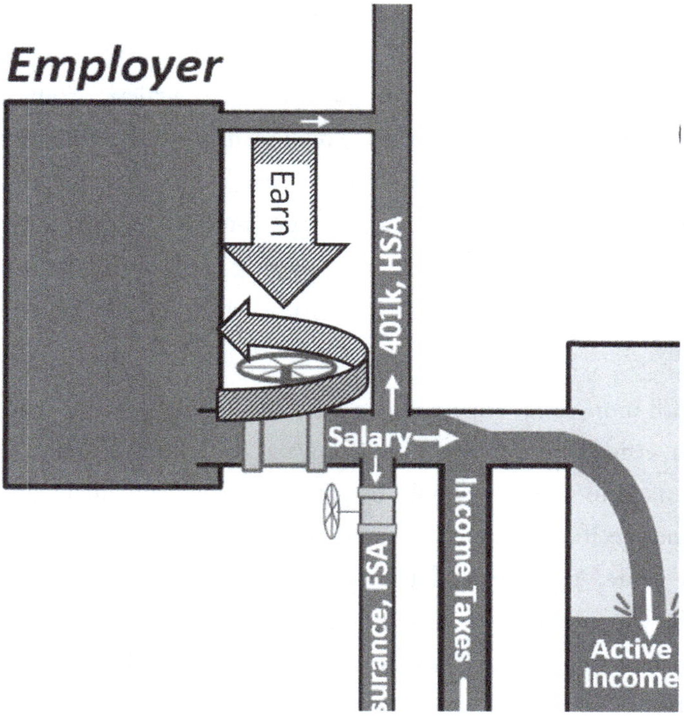
Employer
Earn
401k, HSA
Salary
surance, FSA
Income Taxes
Active
Income

You earn money in exchange for your time and effort. If you are an employee, the obvious method to earning more is to receive a higher salary from your employer, but this can be difficult to achieve. Your salary is based on time, and time is limited. You also may not be able to increase your reach to more people. Therefore, you need to focus on improving the value you provide with the time and scope you have. This means staying competitive in your position by seeking schooling, training, or certifications that may help you perform your job better and more efficiently.

With more skills, consistently negotiate a higher salary to match your gains in efficiency. To do this effectively, you need specific, justified arguments as to why you should be paid more. Ask your manager or boss to outline specific goals and targets for you to meet to get to the next level and pay grade. Also, know what your position is worth in the marketplace to ensure you are not currently underpaid relative to your skills or title. It can also be a good idea to ask for a raise well ahead of any performance review because approvals for salaries take time.

Also, you may get annual raises, but are they keeping up with the cost of living as it increases each year? Typically, there are two types of raises: a merit raise based on performance and a cost of living raise, sometimes referred to as a COLA (Cost of Living Adjustment). Employers often base the COLA on the Consumer Price Index (CPI), which measures annual inflation. Please note that there are national trends and there are also local trends. Sometimes, the cost of living can increase 10% or more in certain areas within one year, while in other areas they only increase 5% during that same year.

Make sure your salary is at least keeping up with the cost of living, there can be an illusion of an increase. If you get a 2% raise while the cost of living increases by 4%, you may feel better than a 2% decrease in salary when the cost of living remains the same. However, in both scenarios you are in the same position.

If you feel stuck, undervalued, or don't see a clear path to higher salaries, it is important to evaluate your options. There are always other employment options out there. While loyalty and integrity are central to a good working relationship, part of knowing what your time and effort are worth is understanding what other employers will pay for them. Your employment will occupy a large part of your life, as seen in the lifetime clock. If you are not satisfied, keep looking and don't settle.

1st Floor Summary: Start with your salary. Earn as much as possible to provide adequate active income. Evaluate your future job prospects. Negotiate your value whenever possible.

The Second Floor: Sacrifice and Save

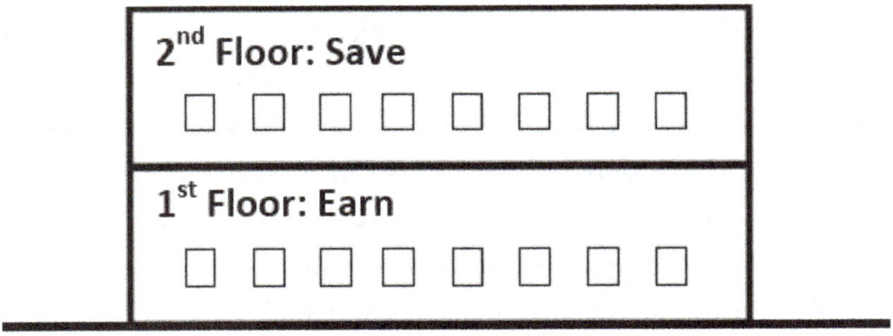

"This natural ventilation system design is not going to work," said the project manager, in front of my boss, no less. "Let's cut it out of the scope and save the money; we need to trim the project's budget."

We were deep into construction, but cost overruns meant we had to find ways to cut scope to reduce cost. The natural ventilation system provided the opportunity for the building occupants to open the windows, allowing fresh air into the space and a way to save air conditioning cost. The system was unique and would be the largest of its type in Southern California and the second largest in the U.S. There had been several similar attempts, many of which ended in failure.

In two years researching and designing the system, I spent countless hours performing computer analyses, calculations, and small-scale testing. I knew it was going to work and be a big win for my team, but I had to convince the project manager not to cut it.

"This natural ventilation system is not required, it is a nice-to-have," the project manager pushed. "Eliminating it will save us a fortune."

"But we've spent thousands designing and engineering the system already; that sunk cost will be lost forever if we let it go now," I said, trying to appeal to his economic side.

"That is water under the bridge. I'm going to the VP to get approval."

I had already convinced my boss, the director, and the rest of the team that the system could work. But I knew the complexities would be over the VP's head and he would probably OK the scope removal. I had to think fast.

"When we started this project, the VP said this project was going to be a premier office work environment. The building is going to not only retain existing talent but attract new talent. No other building around has this system and it is the only defining system left. If we cut it, we are not complying with the VP's original direction."

I continued, feeling his resolve waning. "The system will save us money in the long run. By not running our air conditioning when the windows are open, we will get the money we spent on the system back in 3 years. It will be as if it was free."

"Okay fine, but if this thing doesn't work it's all on you!" he warned.

Success . . . for now.

In the third chapter, when talking about time and money, I discussed opportunity cost. Opportunity cost is what you sacrifice when choosing one option over another.

Hyperbolic discounting is a term given for when offered two similar rewards, humans show a preference for one that arrives sooner rather than later. It is the tendency for people to choose a smaller-sooner reward over a larger-later reward. Smaller-sooner rewards are typically pleasure-related. If you recall, long-term happiness and eudaimonia are self-sustaining happiness stemming from what we give in order to receive happiness in return. Having the right mindset is understanding that saving means sacrificing immediate, short-lived gratification for delayed, but greater prospects.

Saving is about your control over smaller-sooner rewards. However, saving is not just about not spending money. It's also about not losing money. In my back-and-forth with the project manager, he wanted to save money now while I convinced him to not lose money in the future.

You lose money every day to expenses, inflation, taxes, depreciation, and interest. It is very hard to earn money and very easy to lose it. Saving often comes down to accounting—you are likely to waste money if you are not keeping track of it. Knowing where each dollar goes helps identify areas of waste. Accounting also helps you create realistic budgets. In the rest of this chapter, I will discuss expenses, inflation, and taxes. Interest and depreciation will be covered in subsequent chapters.

Expenses

Much of our free time involves consumption. Consumption is central to many activities associated with pleasure. Consumer culture encourages consumption by promising gratification of desires and presenting it as a solution for a variety of problems and as a path to happiness.[17] However, expenses equal money and time down the drain. There are millions of products out there vying for your attention, appealing to your wants, and promising happiness. You don't need most of these. Ego and envy are the biggest risk to savings. Ask yourself, why do you want something? Is it for the happiness promised? Is it for you or is it for someone else's perception of you?

The truth is, other people are not concerned with the things you own. And in fact, possessions can be an obstacle to achieving long-term happiness. The value of consumer goods plummets as soon as you buy them. They can lead to disappointment if you expect owning something lavish will improve your quality of life, only to find out that it doesn't.

This vanity does not increase your net worth. Remember what you learned about using the right mindset to buy your house: understand the opportunity and consider the costs. This same concept applies to your everyday purchases and expenses as well. Money represents your time—spend it wisely.

Some expenses are necessary, and this is where the concept of Utility comes into play. *Utility* is the relative satisfaction and happiness you get from using, owning, or doing something. It is a measurement used by economists to model and study choice; that is given two items, a logical person would choose the item that provides more utility as in value or worth. Based on marginal utility, we all should rationally choose the most efficient use of our money and purchase items that only fulfill their function. This is the rational definition of quality, and, as an engineer, where my utility is maximized. But, as humans, we are not rational. Many prefer form over function and put greater utility in not just how something works, but how it looks or makes us feel.

As discussed, I can't tell you what makes you happy. We all have different ideas of what utility means to us depending on our priorities. But be mindful of what you may classify as quality of life. Buying a watch may bring you utility and happiness, but will buying a gold Rolex for a hundred times more bring you that much more happiness? Warming your house when it is freezing outside during the winter is absolutely necessary. But, cooling your house to a chilly 65°F when it is 100 degrees outside? Excessive.

Even more so than the salary valve, you have control over the flow of money from your Income Tank. To reach financial independence, you need to minimize this stream of expenses as much as possible. You need to turn this valve closed so you can divert your money elsewhere.

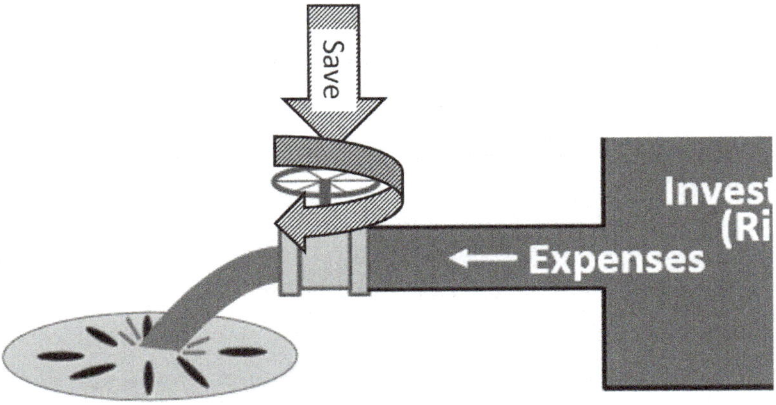

People often wonder how much they should save for investment. The answer is simple: *as much as required to get to your milestone.* Remember, you need to invest $__,____ per year at a rate of return of __% to reach your milestone. To be able to invest that amount, you first need to save up by limiting yourself to only necessary expenses. Until you get to your milestone, you should make every effort to live below your means by spending less—far less—than you earn. This is the short-term sacrifice in pursuit of much longer-term happiness.

However, you must buy some things: groceries, transportation, household consumables, clothes, and other essentials. These are all necessary expenses. Just make sure you are always shopping. Shopping may seem like a bad activity when it comes to financial decisions, but when I say "shop," I mean shopping around: justifying, analyzing, comparing, waiting, negotiating, then buying. These should be the barriers to overcome.

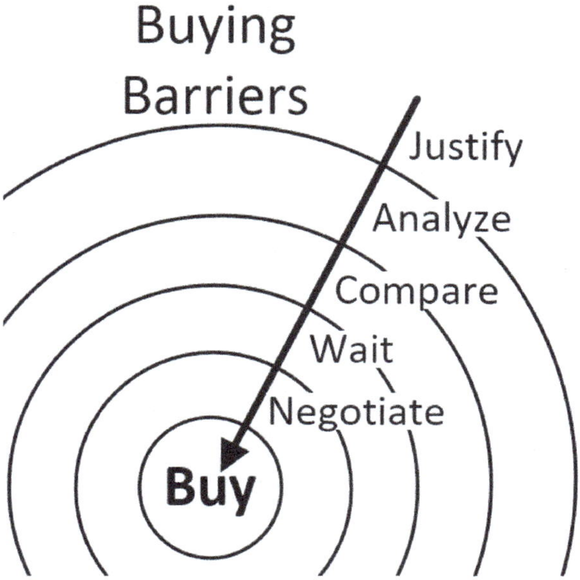

Think of the barriers as walls around the city of buying. You must get through each wall before you reach the center of the city and commit to giving up your hard-earned money.

Some small or repetitive items such as toilet paper or apples may not be worth your time to fully complete each step to analyze the price. That is up to you to decide. To make the decision easier, come up with quick qualifications (price, quality, amount) to determine if an item is worth sacrificing your time to try to get a better deal.

The first barrier is to **JUSTIFY** your purchase. Ask yourself this: Is the money you will spend on this item going to save time at a rate greater than the value of your time? This is an opportunity cost question. What is your time worth to you? If you value your time at $30 per hour, is it worth it to buy something for $60 if it saves you an hour? Can you justify driving an extra 15 minutes to save $5 on gas? Is it worthwhile to pay someone to perform a task for you if you can do it yourself for less?

Finally, the most important justification is: Will this purchase add to your long-term happiness or is this an instant gratification purchase? More to the point, is this a *want* or a *need*? People often buy based on emotions, then justify their actions with altered logic and fact. One way to tell if something is a want or a need is to see where you would stand after the purchase. If the value of the item significantly decreases after you buy it, it's usually a want, not a need.

If you are in the right mindset, your justification will include opportunity costs. However, if you justify buying a $3,000 handbag by saying it only costs $1 per day over 10 years, then you don't understand opportunity costs. If you spend $3,000 on an unnecessary product or service when you could otherwise invest that money for 10 years, then spending the $3,000 would cost you an additional $1,050 in foregone interest earnings. This would bring the real price tag of that handbag to $4,050. So, the question you should ask yourself is: Is what I am spending my money on worth not $3000, but $4,050?

Next, you should **ANALYZE**. Is this purchase a quality product? Will it last for a long time, or is it for single use? Is it more expensive to buy or to make? Looking at the individual parts of an item you may realize that the materials make up only a fraction of the cost. Sometimes you may realize the cost markup over just the material cost is not worth the full purchase price.

Take a hamburger for example. Craft burgers from custom burger restaurants are all the rage these days. You can pay $12, $15 or even $18 dollars for a single burger. But if you break down the ingredients, lettuce, tomato, ground beef, bread, cheese, and egg (if you are adventurous) their total combined cost may be only $3 or $4. Realize you are not just paying for the material and labor to make the hamburger, but for the restaurant's rent, utilities, marketing, insurance, permits, licenses, profits, and even their mistakes, errors, and waste. With all of these costs going into that burger, do you still want to buy it or just make one yourself? Both choices involve your time.

The next barrier your purchase should overcome is to **COMPARE** it against similar products. There are always alternatives and these days online price comparison websites and apps are very good at serving their purpose. Make sure you evaluate competing products before you commit to buying. But don't just look at price. Quality, warranties, return policies, operating costs, and service and support all play a factor in the overall experience and total cost of ownership.

Saving money short term can waste time long term. In the long run, bad quality is expensive. A molded Ikea chair may look nice and cost a fraction of an original Eames chair, but chances are that it breaks in a couple of years and you'll need to buy a new one. Resultantly, you lose money buying bad quality. In the end, you wasted money and, as we now understand, that means you wasted time.[xvi]

Now **WAIT**. If this is a large purchase, then sleep on it. Wait to see if the price drops. Wait to see if your desire changes. Wait to see if a better opportunity arises. There is a human tendency to take a long time to consider small purchasing decisions, but when faced with a large purchase, even analytical people jump in quicker than they should.

Once you have targeted your item, **NEGOTIATE**. Mostly everything is negotiable; you just need to ask. Work with the seller to see how you can get the item for less. Floor model? Refurbished? Any discounts? Even if the price doesn't move, you may be able to get added extras at no cost.

After going through all these steps, you'll know you've made the best deal you could have at that time. For large ticket items you can save a significant amount of money and hopefully you will have made the right choices to keep you on track. The right mindset understands that consumption, particularly conspicuous consumption, rarely brings the happiness promised. Consumption for some is an endless competition where nothing is enough and what other people have is always better. It's an endless race of comparing apparent success.

Sometimes, however, you don't have the luxury of shopping. Accidents happen, and we are forced to spend. That's why it's worth investing in insurance and estate planning. It may seem counterintuitive to spend more on insurance in order to eventually save, but this is a quite necessary expense. Everyone should review this action plan checklist and ensure coverage or a comparable plan of action in all these important areas:

- ☐ Car insurance
- ☐ Health insurance
- ☐ Dental insurance
- ☐ Life insurance
- ☐ Homeowner's (or renter's) insurance
- ☐ Umbrella liability insurance
- ☐ Long-term disability (LTD) insurance
- ☐ Estate plan
- ☐ Living trust
- ☐ Pour-over will
- ☐ Advanced healthcare and physician directives
- ☐ Healthcare and financial power of attorney
- ☐ Beneficiary designations for all accounts
- ☐ Contingent beneficiaries

☐ Long-term care

While I don't include all the details of these protections, I encourage you to research each one and become familiar with their purpose. One note of caution: safeguard your hard-earned savings, but don't overpay on your coverage. All these necessary items can be analyzed, compared, and negotiated, so shop around.

Taxes

Taxes are unavoidable but can be limited. How much you pay is under your control. Tax rules are complex, ever-changing, and intricate. However, if you understand the basic policies and use this understanding to limit your tax liability, you can save a significant amount. But don't feel you need to go at it alone. To not miss any major tax breaks, you should hire someone to help you plan and file your taxes. A CPA or EA can help with the intricacies of tax preparation at year end. But, during the year, your financial decisions impact your end of year taxable amounts and should always be on your mind. This section will cover the three major taxes: income tax, sales tax, and capital gains tax, and how to visualize and limit their impact on your financial flow.

Income Taxes

Remember that with a higher salary comes higher income taxes. To limit your income taxes, you have two optional diversions: retirement plans and health insurance/FSA plans.

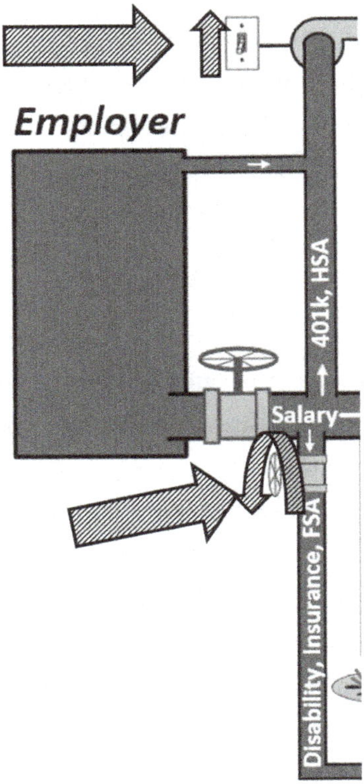

One of the best, most direct, and easiest ways to pay your future self is to maximize your contributions to your employer's 401(k) plan, if you have one available to you. There are many reasons why this is the best way to meet your financial independence milestone.

Salary diverted to a 401(k) is pre-tax. That means it is taken out of your paycheck before income taxes are calculated and withdrawn. This step reduces your taxable income. Yes, you will not make as much short-term net income if you max out your 401(k) each year, but you'll reduce your income taxes, which is a worthwhile long-term adjustment that will bring your milestone of financial independence that much closer.

Most employers match some percentage of 401(k) contributions. This is free money—take it, don't pass it over.

The dividends and capital gains from holdings in your retirement accounts are tax-deferred. By maxing out your 401(k), you are completely avoiding two separate taxable events and putting money directly into your Asset Tank. By using this money to invest wisely in assets that appreciate in value, your total net worth can freely exponentiate.

Please note that while 401(k)s are tax-advantaged, they are not completely tax free. Once you reach the age of 59½, you can start withdrawing funds from your 401(k) account, and those withdrawals will be taxed as income. However, you can manage and have control over those withdrawals along with your income to keep your effective income tax rate low.

There is another tax-advantaged account type that is not shown in the Financial Flow Diagram but is important to discuss. It is a Roth IRA. A Roth is similar to a 401(k) account because money earned in the account is not taxed, but money invested into the account must be post-tax money. The benefit of a Roth comes during retirement when you don't have to pay income taxes on withdrawals as you would with a 401(k).

Health insurance and flexible savings accounts (FSAs) use pre-tax money to reduce your expenses. Money diverted into these systems is an efficient use of your salary, however, there are limits and terms in these accounts that are important to understand. These limits are detailed and depend on your choice of plan and provider. I won't go into all the requirements here, but I highly recommend using the resources available to you to find the best way to take advantage of your health insurance and FSA tax-advantaged options.

Sales Tax

Sales tax is a tax paid to a governing body for the sale of certain goods and services. It is unavoidable in many situations. But to limit the sales tax you pay, understand that sales tax is usually imposed on assets that depreciate, compounding an overall loss in your total net worth.

You have control over the sales tax valve by controlling what types of assets you buy.

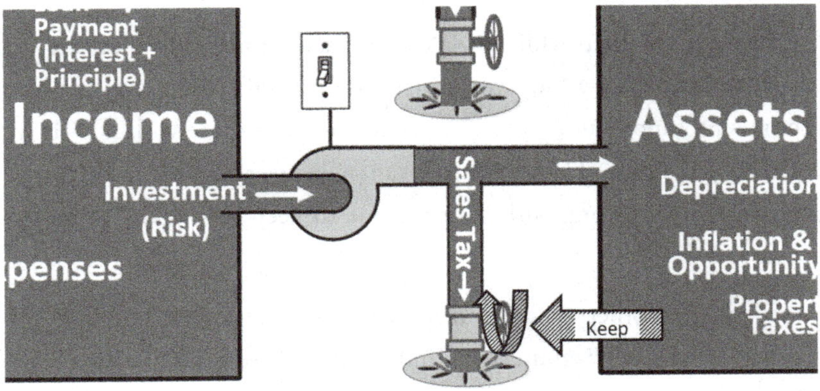

Keep the money that you have worked so hard to earn by buying more assets that appreciate and do not carry sales tax requirements. Assets such as stocks, bonds, and mutual funds do not carry sales tax. In addition, some states either exempt or discount items from sales tax. To limit your sales tax on potentially taxable items, try shopping online and look for retailers that are not required to charge sales tax. It may also be worth the trip to travel to a state that has no sales tax if you're planning a large purchase. Finally, shopping for used items at garage sales or on online exchanges like Craigslist is ideal because you will get the discount of buying a secondhand item without having to pay sales tax.

Capital Gains Tax

Capital gains are profits realized from the sale of assets. The amount of tax is based on the amount of asset's value appreciation from the time it was bought to the time it is sold. The amount of tax is also based on the amount of time the asset is held and the type of asset. While capital gains tax is related to passive income, it is still a type of income tax. However, compared to income tax related to your salary, you have greater control over lowering your capital gains tax.

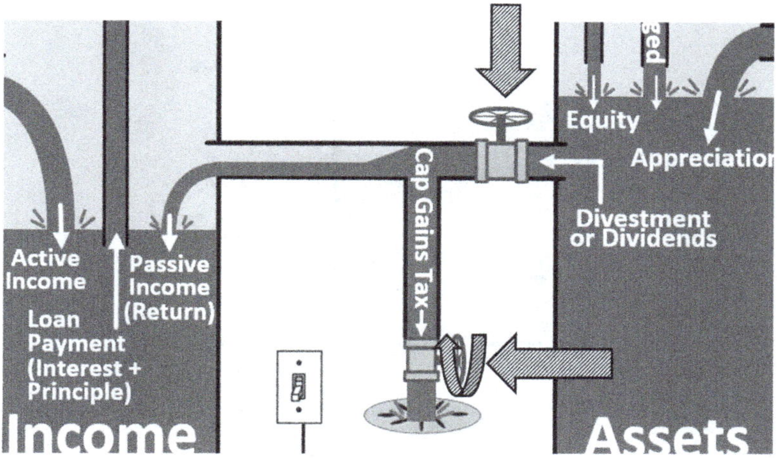

Capital gains taxes from stocks can be either long-term or short-term. If you sell a stock less than a year after you buy it, you will be charged a short-term capital gains tax rate, which is equal to your income tax rate, as is your salary. However, if you hold a stock for longer than a year, you will be charged at the lower, long-term Federal capital gains tax rate of 15% when you sell it. Depending on your effective tax rate this lower rate could result in a 35% savings. In addition, income from "qualified" stock dividends are taxed at the long-term capital gains tax.

Another tax-advantaged asset is a municipal bond also known as 'munis'. A muni is an interest-bearing, fixed-income bond (debt obligation) issued by a state or local municipality. These bond's interest paid is exempt from federal taxes and sometimes state and local taxes as well.

Whole books are written on tax-saving strategies. I am just scratching the surface; there are plenty more tax strategies out there. I encourage you to become familiar with your current and future tax liabilities as this is a major impact on your overall net worth.

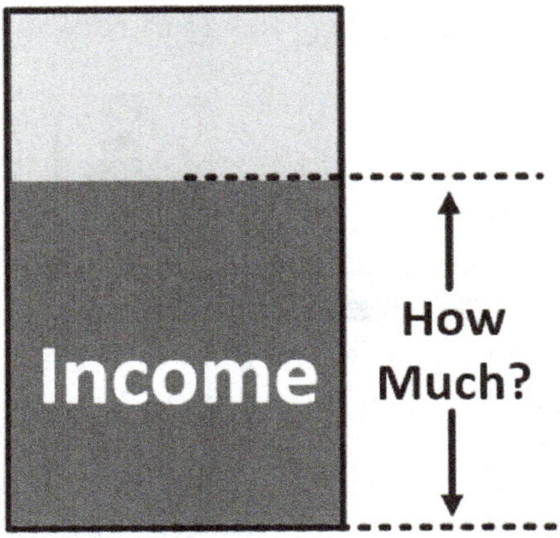

Saving by following the recommendations in this chapter will increase the level in your Income Tank, but how much do you need to keep in your Income Tank for emergencies and for a "rainy day" fund? Cash left in your bank is losing value to inflation and opportunity, but it's recommended to keep a minimum of six months' worth of expenses in readily available (liquid) cash for potential short-term, high-expense, or low-income events such as a job loss. Of course, you must keep accurate accounting records of your personal finances and cash flow to know exactly how much, in dollar terms, six months of expenses is for you and your family. If you look back at the tanks, assume that you have completely closed your salary valve. How long would the money in your Income Tank last?

As discussed, inflation is the increase in prices over time and is a constant drain on all your tanks. Opportunity cost is the money that you miss out on when you hold onto your income rather than putting it to good use in an easy, safe investment. There is no avoiding these costs. You can only make sure their effects are minimized. Holding on to uninvested large amounts of cash, or investing in assets that depreciate, increases your exposure to inflation and opportunity cost.

The risk of holding that six months' worth of cash, uninvested, is the impact of inflation and opportunity. If your emergency fund is $15,000, you are losing almost $1,000 of value every year by just letting it sit in the bank. However, the risk of not having that money in an emergency outweighs the risk of loss due to inflation and opportunity. The good news is that there are other options, such as a HELOC if you own a house, discussed in later chapters, to give you access to an emergency fund.

Keeping any more than six months of expenses in an emergency fund for an extended period is money down the drain. Saving money for a planned investment is one justification for having extra cash. But spare, uninvested money results in an expense that will not help you reach your milestone.

Having a right mindset includes saving your earnings. Saving is about both not spending and avoiding unplanned expenses. Saving money, now gives you opportunity to use your money for your future. Think hard about your current cash flow drains. Is that money going down the expenses, taxes and deprecation drains really contributing to your long-term happiness? If not, then let's divert it to something that does.

2nd Floor Summary: Save as much as you can by reducing expenses, taxes, and exposure to inflation. Only spend on expenses that contribute to long-term happiness.

The Third Floor: Borrow for Tomorrow

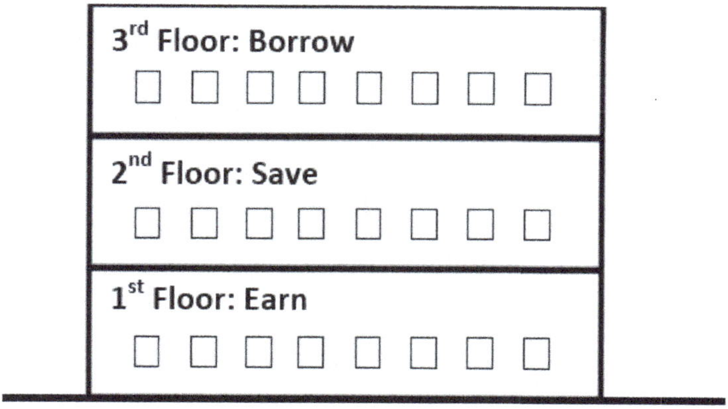

After one year into our marquee project, things were going well. The construction of the primary building was on schedule and under budget, even with the unique natural ventilation system.

The project also included a new amenities building on the other side of the site. This building was to house a cafeteria, theater, meeting rooms, and a medical office space. The second building was about one year behind the first and still in design. We figured the design of this smaller building would be easier, but that did not turn out to be the case.

"This architect is killing me; they won't let me put the necessary mechanical equipment anywhere," our consultant said, speaking about this smaller, adjacent amenities building. "We are supposed to keep the roof clear of any equipment and they won't give me any space in the inside or around the perimeter. There is nowhere else to put the air conditioning system."

We brainstormed for over an hour. What about the garage? No room. What about the main building? Too far. What about a secret underground lair, like a Batcave?

"I like it, but maintenance access may be an issue," I pointed out sarcastically.

Then I had an idea. "I know," I said eagerly. "Instead of building a new system, let's borrow air conditioning from the adjacent building."

"Do they have the capacity?" the consultant asked.

"Yes, we just upgraded their plant last year," I stated.

"If we are borrowing the air conditioning, what will they get in return?" he asked.

"A very clean building with no mechanical system to look at!" I joked.

Earning and saving are the two base floors of your right mindset building. They support everything above. Borrowing is the third floor and is related to saving. Just as I was saving our project a large cost and headaches by borrowing from the adjacent building, your money can be saved in borrowing. Interest operates as an expense: it flows out and does not come back in. Saving on interest payments when borrowing is the focus of this section.

Borrowing using a right mindset is all about avoiding the hidden opportunity costs of paying interest. Recall, opportunity cost is the price you pay when you give up something to get something else. Avoiding opportunity cost is about being as efficient with your money as possible. When you borrow money, you are paying someone else's opportunity costs via interest. And with debt comes the risk of borrowing at an interest rate that is too high.

It took me and my consultant a long time to find a solution to our problem that was reasonable. In this chapter, you'll learn about the factors that determine if an interest rate is reasonable.

Debt is money that a borrower owes to a lender. Interest is the fee that a borrower pays to a lender for taking on the risk of the loan. Interest is calculated as a percentage of the outstanding principal. The percentage is the interest rate, generally paid periodically.

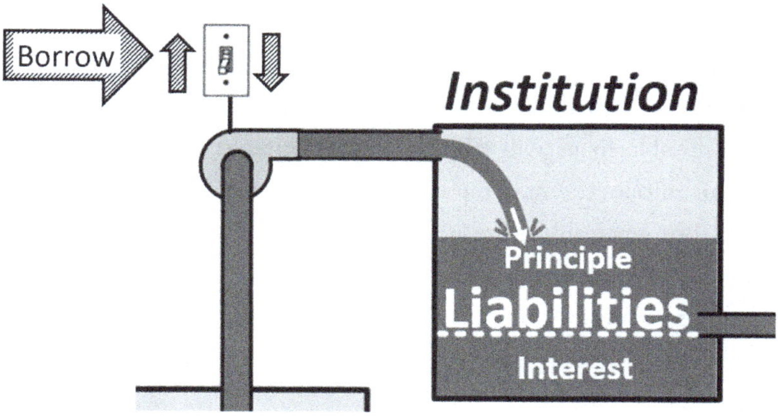

Not all debt is the same. As discussed before, there is good debt and bad debt. In general, good debt is a low interest loan used to buy an appreciating asset. Bad debt is high interest loans used for depreciating assets. A more detailed description is: Good debt is used to purchase an asset that appreciates in value at a higher rate than the interest rate so that at the end of the loan, your Asset Tank was filled more than your Income Tank was drained.

However, it's a bit more complicated than that. Let's say you get a loan to buy a car with a low interest rate. The car will depreciate; there's no question about that. If you must choose between paying the full value upfront or taking a loan with a lower rate than what you could make by investing the amount of the loan in stocks or bonds, then it may be more beneficial to take the low-interest loan. This way, you can put the money that would otherwise be spent outright to work in your favor in other investments. This is a good example of avoiding opportunity cost. You are choosing to take the opportunity of a positive difference in interest and investment rates.

It is also important to understand the difference between a fixed-rate and an adjustable or variable-rate loan. With fixed-interest rate loans, the interest rate is set when you take out the loan and will not change. With an adjustable-rate loan, also known as adjustable-rate mortgages (ARMs) the interest rate may go up or down throughout the duration of the loan. Many adjustable loans will start at a lower interest rate than fixed-rate loans. This initial rate may stay the same for months, one year, or even a few years. But when this introductory period is over, your interest rate will change, and the amount of your payment is likely to go up. If you must use an adjustable-rate loan, it is crucial to understand when the rate will adjust and if the loan is still advantageous if the rate and payment reach the maximums per the loan contract.

This is not to say that adjustable rate loans are all bad, especially if the payoff period is short; they can minimize the risk of quickly rising rates. Fixed rates are higher than variable rates, just like buying insurance is more expensive than not buying insurance. Both buy down your risk but come at a cost.

Sometimes your best investment can be paying off debts—especially bad debts. Making mistakes and incurring too much bad debt is a burden, but not an inescapable one. It's important to have an accurate accounting of your money flow so that you have clear figures that describe your gains and any money pits developing bad debts. This ensures you are better prepared to make positive, proactive choices when working on your right mindset.

You have just read about the rainy-day fund, also known as an emergency fund. Having six months' worth of readily accessible money is recommended for unplanned events, such as a layoff or a large medical bill, but holding that money uninvested means you're missing out on returns. One option to fill your need for a six-month cushion without having a large amount of cash on hand is to look at getting approved for—but not using—a home equity loan, which is a lump-sum loan with a fixed term and rate. Another option to consider is a home equity line of credit (HELOC), which features variable rates and continuing access to funds.

These loans are collateralized, depend on the amount of equity in your home, and generally require a new appraisal. A home equity loan might be a good loan if you anticipate a large one-time expense such as a wedding, the purchase of a second home, or debt consolidation. A fixed rate and predictable monthly payment can help you budget as you work toward your financial goals. A HELOC is good if you need extra money intermittently as you can access the available funds as you need them.

With these borrowing options in place, an unplanned event can be financed instead of paid for with your savings. However, there are some critical things to consider. You must pledge your home as collateral, which means if you don't make payments, your property could go through foreclosure. Also, your credit score could be affected if you miss payments. Most importantly, by borrowing money to pay for an unexpected event, you'll have to pay interest on the loan, and that interest rate may be more than what you would have gained by investing the money.

Realize that when you buy something with a loan, it is not yours. You only gain ownership after the full debt is paid off. Critical to knowing if a debt will be good or bad is understanding the interest rate and whether it is fixed or adjustable. When you borrow money, you are making a time-value determination. You are determining that your purchase using borrowed money is more valuable now than a larger amount of future dollars due to the interest you will pay and the opportunity you will have lost.

To be clear, I am not saying you must borrow to reach financial independence. Not all paths to financial independence are paved through increased liabilities. However, understanding when and what to borrow can help you build the right mindset. Now, let's move on to my favorite floor of the building, investing our saved money.

3rd Floor Summary: Borrow as needed, but only when the rate of interest is less than what you would lose to inflation. Liabilities are responsibilities, so choose wisely when taking on debt.

The Fourth Floor: Invest Like the Best

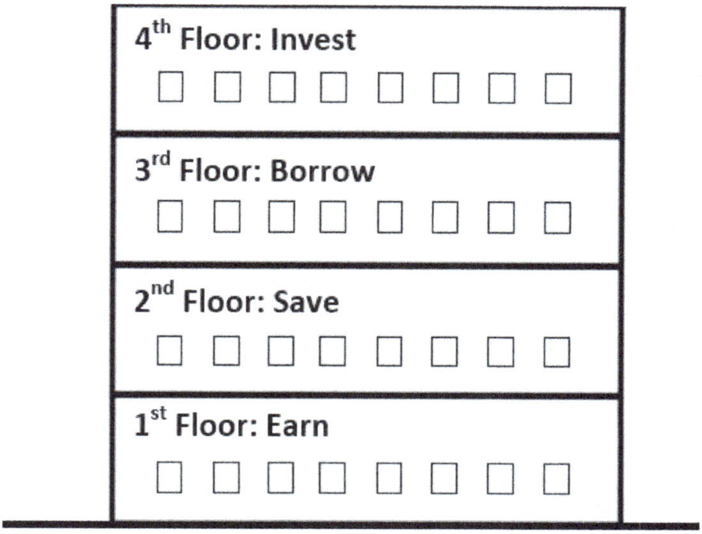

Every construction project presents challenges. Ours was no different. Construction teams must have the resolve to face these challenges repeatedly as they come up. Multi-year projects test the patience of even the best teams. After eighteen months into our project, everyone was exhausted. We were closer to the end than the beginning. We had dodged curveballs and overcome many tribulations.

It was a Tuesday. I came into my office and greeted my coworker. They wasted little time to drop the bomb.

"Our project manager has been let go."

"I'm sorry, did you say the project manager has been fired?" I asked incredulously.

"Yes."

"Really!? Now? We are waist-deep into this thing," I said. "Why were they let go?"

"They won't say, but something went down and the manager had to take the fall. Their replacement is taking over today."

"Great, so we invested all of that time and effort into getting the project manager on our side and now we have to start again with the new one," I lamented.

"It's not as bad as you think. The replacement is also a good project manager. We have ensured the right decisions have been made; now we just have to get over one more hurdle and it will be smooth sailing," my coworker assured.

I hoped he was right. It seemed very risky to bring in someone new at this point. But with this risk, would there be a reward?

"Can I keep my hard hat and work boots when they come for me?" I said flippantly.

"No way, I'm putting those up for sale!" my coworker shot back facetiously.

As with our marquee project, to get to this point you have invested a significant amount of time to build up a great foundation and stack more on top of your mindset. Now we go higher up into investing for the future. Investing is the fourth floor of the right mindset building, and, from here, I can see the happiness horizon.

You do not *save* for retirement, as the saying goes; you *invest* for retirement. Every time you buy items that have resale value, you are investing. This means you're buying assets that you expect will appreciate in value over time and selling those assets only when the time is right. Envisioning everything as an investment with an expected return is an important part of having the right mindset. This is key to reaching the financial independence milestone.

Investing with the right mindset using our Financial Flow Diagram is about buying assets (using our pump) that have a high probability of appreciating in value over time and divesting or collecting dividends as a way to boost our passive income stream.

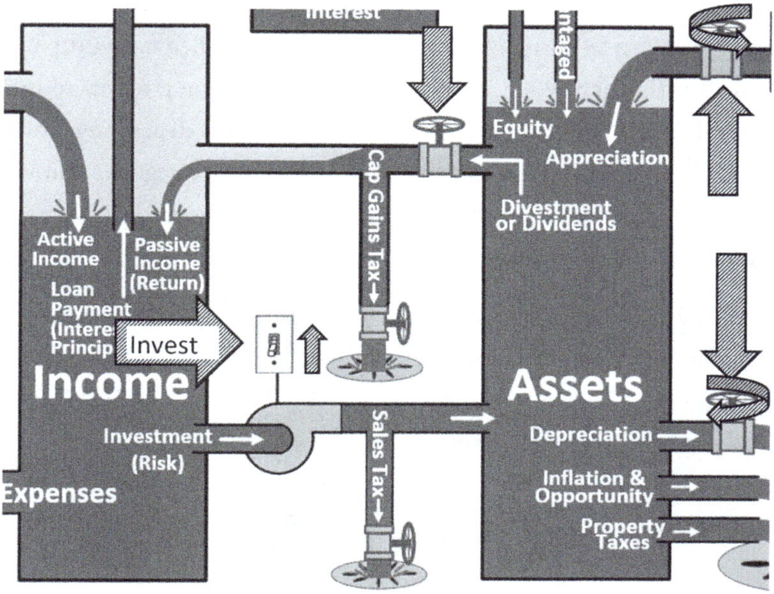

For most people, the first word that comes to mind when thinking about investing is *risk*. Investing is perceived as being risky, and it is. All investments are considered to be a risk, but so is all the money in your Financial Flow Diagram. All of your income, assets, and liabilities are at risk of loss, even the money you keep in the bank. When your fear of this potential loss is greater than your desire to gain, you experience loss aversion, which can be avoided if you understand the difference in the probability and size of loss, depending on where your money is kept.

The reality is that it's riskier to *not* take good investment risks than it is to invest wisely. It's important to make planned investments with calculated risks and keep your calculated returns. Losing money is always hard, but working hard, investing time and energy, and losing it all to a bad investment is the hardest loss of all.

From the Plan and Schedule chapter, you know that to get to financial independence by your scheduled target date, you need to invest $__,___ per year at a rate of return of _%. The planned amount per year is achieved through your earning and saving. The rate of return is achieved through investing. That rate is up to you, depending on your choice of investments. Investments come in general categories known as 'classes'. Asset classes are plentiful and include stocks, bonds, mutual funds, real estate, and certificates of deposit, among others.

All investments carry risk, but will the return be worth it? You may come across a risk triangle that looks like this:

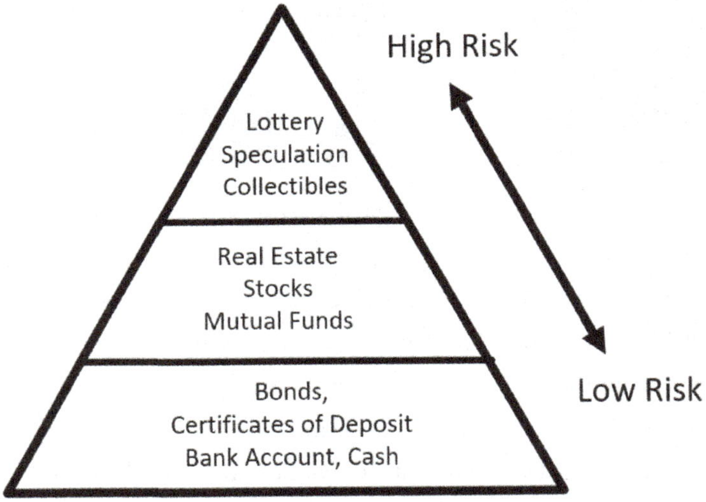

If you look at this graphic, you may infer that one should keep or invest most of their money in low-risk asset classes such as cash and bonds because they occupy the largest section of the triangle. Unfortunately, this is misleading and misunderstood.

You need to not only consider risk, but also the potential financial reward in line with your expected return. There is always risk, but whenever you invest in an asset, you are taking on additional risk. Over time, that asset will appreciate or depreciate in value. When you choose to sell that asset, you will either return a gain from appreciation or a loss from depreciation.

If you sell for a gain, you'll collect a positive return for the original investment risk you took. However, if you sell for a loss, your return will be negative. The right mindset is as follows: *When investing, there is always risk and there is always a return—it's just not always a reward.*

Before going any further, let's define the terms *risk*, *reward*, and *return*.

Risk is easy to understand (and overestimate), but difficult to quantify. Risk is the uncertainty of future consequences due to the choices you make in the present. Many equate *risk* with *loss,* but this is not true. Risk is the *potential* for a return of a loss or a return of less than what you expected. Actual loss is the realization of that negative potential. This potential is defined by both the probability and the amount of loss. Complicating the quantification further, the potential amount of loss is not always equal to the investment amount. Investing is not like gambling, wherein the amount you bet is always equal to the amount you could lose. More on this later.

Modern theories formulate risk based on complex factors, including volatility, beta, standard deviation, variance, and others to calculate a very precise number for investors. However, true risk is an estimation and, just like happiness, will be different for everyone. You may have heard of or taken risk tolerance questionnaires that measure how much you identify with statements such as "I prefer investments with little or no fluctuation in price." The problem with this statement is that risk is not equal to price fluctuations or volatility. Volatility is not risk when you are diversified and you have a long-term investment horizon. Risk is the possibility of permanent loss or inadequate return. You only take a loss if you sell lower than you bought. If you are never forced to sell at inopportune times when the asset is worth less than when you bought it, you never lose.

Deliberate and strategized risk-taking is a part of self-improvement and personal growth. By recognizing the higher-level consequences of our actions we can take advantage of the opportunities provided to us. I believe risk tolerance is a person's self-perceived ability to stick to an investment plan when their preconceived notions and intuitions are disrupted. It is not just volatility; it is both the willingness and financial capacity to dedicate money to an unknown future. When we buy an asset, we trade the present value for the risk of owning that asset. We are trading our present happiness for the potential for greater future happiness.

Risk tolerance is a delayed gratification mindset. Everyone has loss aversion, but the knowledge and acceptance that bad things are bound to happen when you try something new is the key to growth.

In summary, potential for a loss (risk) is a combination of five factors:

1. **Amount**: How much money are you risking? This is not how much you are investing, but how much could you lose in the worst-case loss scenario.

2. **Probability**: What is the probability of this worst-case loss?

3. **Time**: How much time do you plan to keep your money in the investment? Time affects investments in two ways. The longer you leave

money in an investment, the more likely it will return your expected amount. However, this also results in more risk from inflation and opportunity costs. The time it takes to sell an asset (liquidity) is also a risk.

4. **Fees**: How much do you have to pay for this investment? This includes your time and expenses.

5. **Expectations**: What return do you expect from this investment?

A *reward* is something that might be given in return for a risk taken. Just like risk, reward is not a gain; reward is the *potential* for a gain. Just because you are taking a risk does not mean you will get a reward.

The potential return of a gain (reward) is a combination of three factors:

1. **Amount**: How much do you expect to make? This is not how much you *could* make; it is how much a typical investment in that asset class makes.

2. **Probability**: What is the probability that you will make this amount of money?

3. **Tax**: Subtract the amount of tax you will have to pay to realize your gain.

Return is the result of your investment risk. Return is the net difference between your total amount investment in an asset and total amount received after selling the asset. Your return could be a gain (reward/positive return) or a loss (negative return). Again, everything you do with your money is a risk. Return is what happens to your money.

You may have heard the term "risk-reward" to sum up the relationship between an investment risk you took and the financial reward (if there was one) on your return. Let's see what this looks like if you try to visualize risk, reward, and return.

Risk is the uncertainty of future consequences due to your choices in the present. Your present choice in this example is investing or buying an asset. Over time, that asset's market value could increase, decrease, or fluctuate wildly as in the example below.

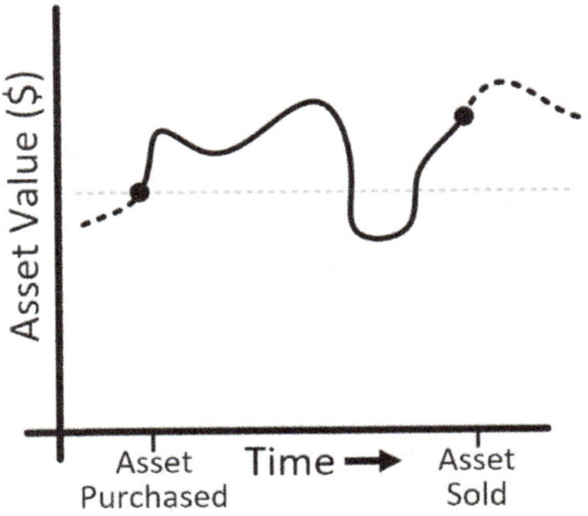

Starting from the present and looking into the future, you know an asset's market value changes over time. With that expectation comes the uncertainty of future value, with an equal chance of selling the asset for a gain or a loss.

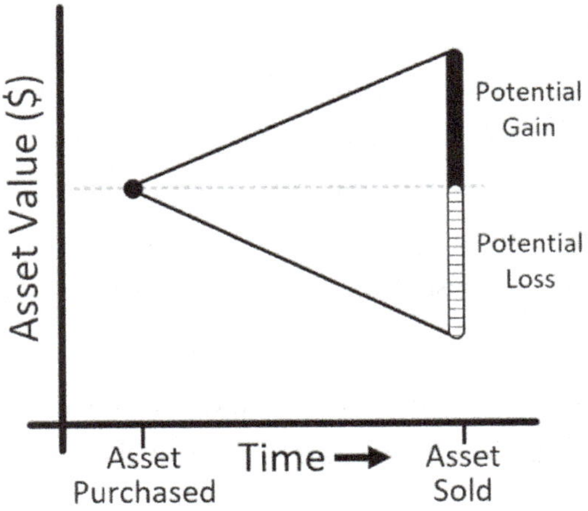

Going back to the definitions, risk is the potential for a return of a loss or a return of less than what you expected. Reward is your potential for a gain, regardless of your expectations. This means risk and reward *overlap*. If you bought a stock and expected a 7% return but sold it for a 5% return, you realized a reward, but the investment underperformed your expectations. This turned out to be risky because if you'd known of the future outcome, you may have used the opportunity to invest in something else. The uncertainty of future performance is an investment risk you must take.

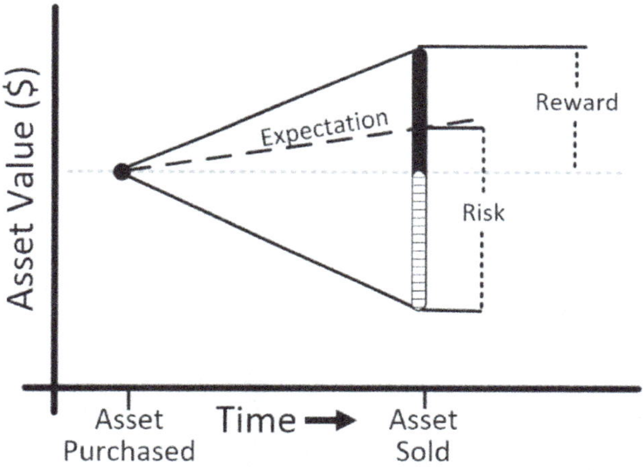

Along with the possibility of a gain or a loss comes the probability of an asset's future market value. Research, knowledge, and understanding help investors determine the probability of future market value. Matching your expectations to the asset's probable future value helps lower risk. Quality assets with a high probability of appreciating will have a low probability of experiencing a loss. The lower the potential for a loss, the lower the risk.

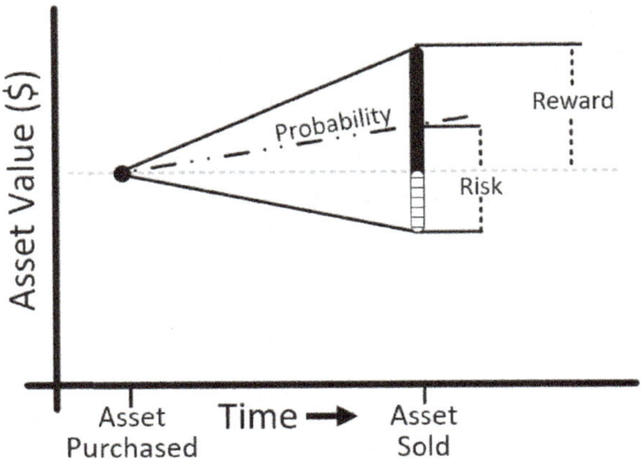

Below is a chart that plots two different asset classes on a line of equal investment. Above the line represents the potential gain of that investment, and below the line represents its potential loss. One asset class is low risk and the other is high risk.

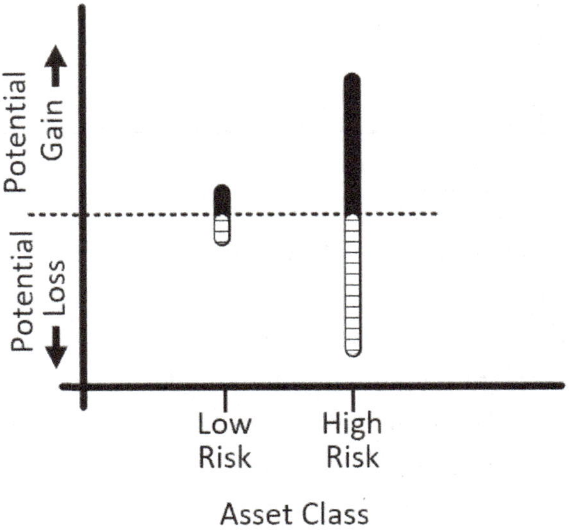

What is often incorrectly understood is that the potential return on investments have an equal amount of risk and reward—that an investment is either low risk/low reward, or high risk/high reward.

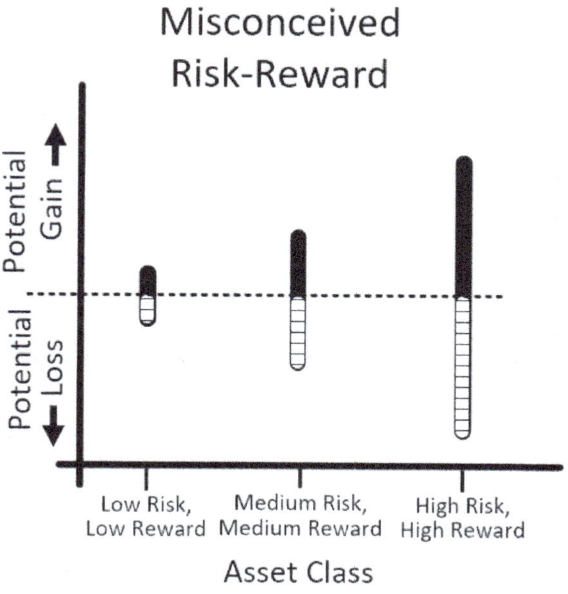

This is not reality. The relationship between risk and reward is not linear. Unfortunately, the popular saying "the higher the risk, the higher the reward" is deceptive. It implies that only large, risky investments will result in large gains. It also implies there will always be a reward.

In reality, there are low-risk investments that have high rewards and high-risk investments that have negative rewards. This disproportionality is why it is important for you to have the right mindset to understand the definitions and relationships between risk and reward for all asset classes. I believe that instead of risk-reward, the term should be risk-reward/no reward/negative reward, or, more simply, *risk-return.*

The key to understanding risk-return is understanding these probabilities and how the different asset classes fit in the spectrum. Each asset class can be generalized into unique return potential ratios. Here is a more detailed chart for visualization of that potential:

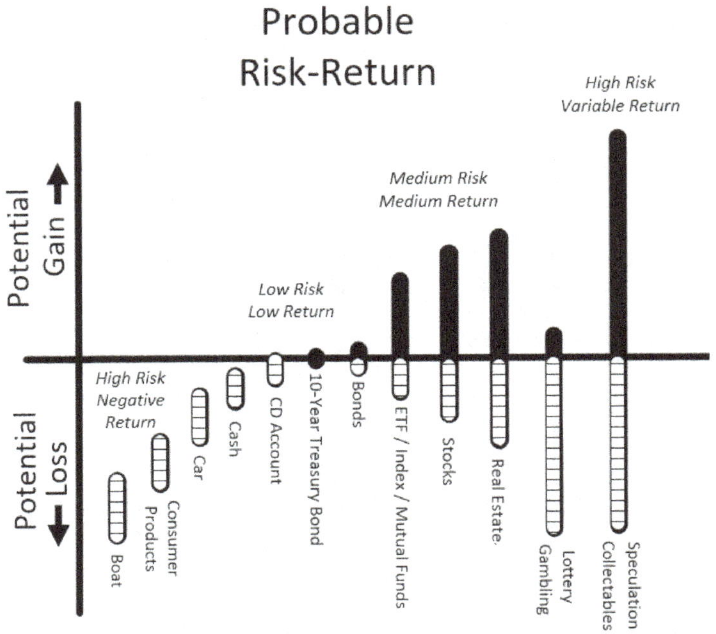

It is important to review your whole income and asset portfolio and review holdings and investments based on risk and return potential. In investing, you often hear about diversity. Yes, you need to be diversified within your types of investments, but *you also need to be diversified in your risk and return potential.* When we link this graphic back to the Financial Flow Diagram, we see how assets that have more potential to return a gain are ones more likely to appreciate and fill your Asset Tank. Assets that have more potential to return a loss are those more likely to depreciate and drain your Asset Tank.

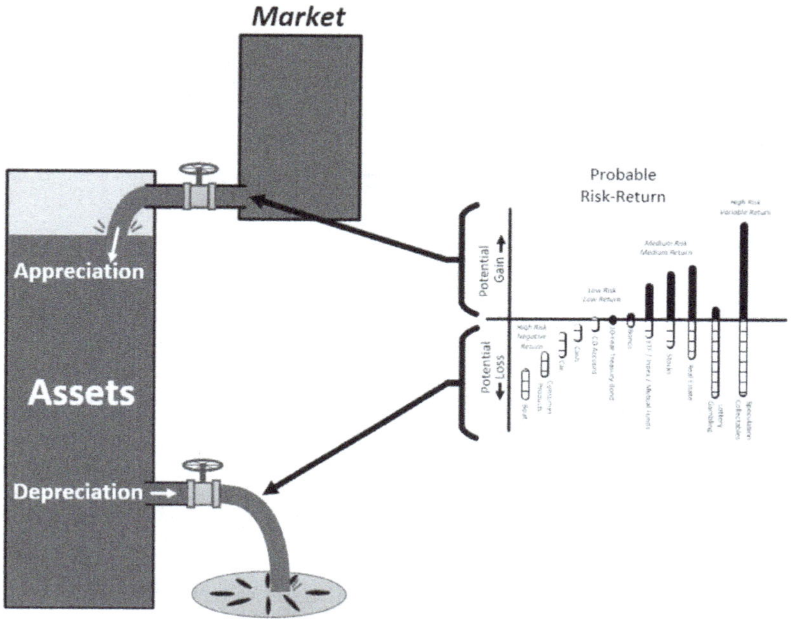

Asset classes such as stocks and real estate are considered risky investments compared to just holding on to cash in a bank. While they have a greater potential for loss, that loss is far outweighed by the potential gain. By being selective and only purchasing assets that have a low probability of depreciating, you can reduce your risk of loss. In addition, you can significantly lower the risk of any investment by doing your research and gaining as much information as you can about the asset.

Over the next few sections, we will look at the four main risk-return categories and the types of asset classes common to each.

High Risk – Negative Return:

Buying Boats, Consumer Products, and Cars

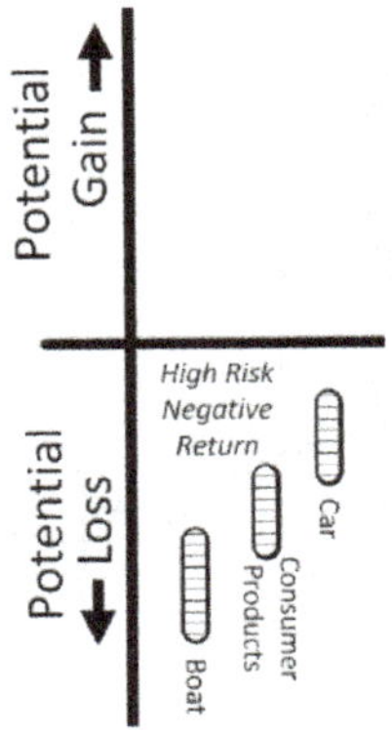

High risk/negative return assets are ones that have a high likelihood of depreciation with no chance of a reward.

Boats are one example I include here as an asset that has a high potential of loss. I don't intend to pick on boat owners, as recreational vehicles (RVs) or trailers could be included here as well. However, of the three, boats typically depreciate more rapidly and carry a higher cost of operation, insurance, and maintenance. They are expensive, hard to sell, and carry high fees.

There is a 100% probability you will lose money on this type of investment. However, this does not affect your probability of being happy spending time on your boat, RV, trailer, or other recreational toy. Don't let me dissuade you from realizing your happiness. Just make sure you understand and can justify the opportunity cost of total toy ownership.

Consumer product assets such as electronics, clothing, jewelry, and other accessories also carry a negative return. The rate of innovation means electronics become obsolete within a few years. Boats may carry some resale value, but electronics can quickly depreciate to zero. Used clothes, jewelry, and accessories are usually passed down or donated, not resold. Again, there is 100% probability you will lose money in these investments.

Cars are a third asset class of bad investments. Transportation is a need. We all need to get around, and—depending on where you live—cars are the most efficient method. If you live outside of a big city, a car saves you time over public transportation, and your time has value. But that value is up to you. A $10,000 used car can transport you just as well as a $50,000 new car.

The risk of loss in the car example includes the total cost of the car plus insurance, maintenance, taxes, fees, and any financing interest. It is an absolute certainty that you will lose some, if not most, of this money to depreciation. The amount of time you hold on to the car affects its lost value. For this example, let's assume you purchase a new car and keep it for the U.S. national average of six years. Six years of probable depreciation, inflation, expenses, and fees can add up to more than 50% value reduction from the initial total cost.

Cars, boats, and other consumable assets are high risk/negative reward investments. Depreciation and inflation continually eat into their value, and there is a low probability of any financial gain after using them. Review the buying barriers from the Second Floor section and seriously consider the opportunity costs before making these purchases.

Low Risk – Low Return:

Holding Cash, CDs, Treasury Bonds, and Corporate Bonds

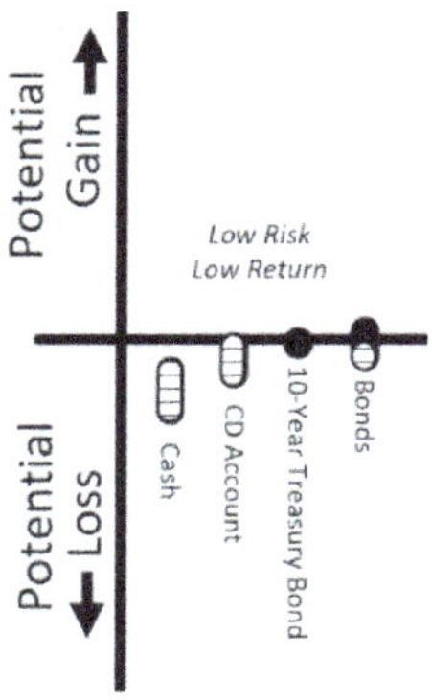

Low risk/low reward assets are ones that will depreciate, but at a known and manageable amount and may provide a slight reward.

You may think that holding cash is a zero-risk option, but it isn't. There are no zero-risk options. Cash can be stolen, lost, or destroyed, and inflation will slowly but surely eat away at its value. Therefore, it is riskier, in the long run, to avoid taking risks. There is no reward for holding onto extra cash.

Another investment in the same low risk/low reward category includes CD accounts. A CD is a certificate of deposit, which is a type of savings account found at banks and credit unions that pays a set interest rate on money deposited. In exchange, you agree to keep the full deposit in the account for a set term. This rate is usually less than the rate of inflation, so in the long term you are still losing money, but maybe at a lower rate than just holding cash.

Next up are 10-year Treasury bonds (also known as bills or notes). This is a debt obligation issued by the United States government with a maturity of 10 years upon initial issuance. A 10-year Treasury bond pays interest at a fixed rate once every six months and pays the face value to the holder at maturity. It is considered "risk-free" because it is backed by the full faith and credit of the U.S. government. The rate the Treasury bond pays out is very important because it is the proxy against which all other investment opportunities are compared. This is the rate the Time Value of Money uses for the opportunity cost basis. Any other choice you make with your money must be compared against this opportunity for a risk-free rate of return.

Lastly, let's talk about bonds, which are commonly referred to as "fixed income securities" (that is, they pay at a fixed rate). When companies, governments, or other entities need to raise money to finance new projects, maintain ongoing operations, or refinance existing debts, they may issue bonds.

All these investments have a lower risk and better return than the ones in the previous section, but these investments may not keep up with your discount rate (inflation + opportunity).

Medium Risk – Medium Return:

Funds, Stocks, and Real Estate

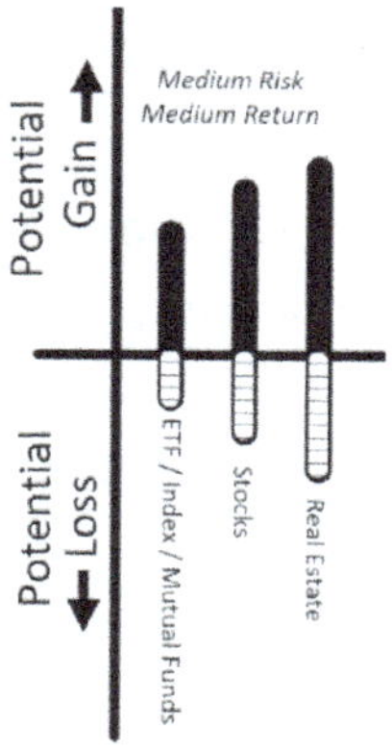

Medium risk/medium reward investments are the most financially efficient place to keep your money. They are most likely to appreciate and provide a reward. These investments include real estate, stocks, mutual funds, exchange traded funds (ETFs), and index funds.

A fund (mutual fund, ETF, or index fund) is an investment vehicle made up of a pool of money collected from many investors for the purpose of investing in securities such as stocks, bonds, money market instruments, and other assets. Some, like mutual funds, are operated by professional money managers, who actively trade investments to produce capital gains for the fund's investors. Others, like ETFs and index funds, are passively managed and carry lower fees than actively managed funds. Funds have an efficient risk-return profile because of the variable amount of investment and the higher probability of a positive return with a longer investment time.

Stocks (also known as "shares" or "equity") are securities that carry ownership in a corporation and represent claims on part of the corporation's assets and earnings. Stocks have a higher risk-return profile than funds because they are not as diversified, but they're similar because of the variable amount of investment required.

Real estate is ownership of land and any buildings or natural resources (like crops, minerals, or water) on it. When buying real estate, many typically pay 20% of the property's total cost upfront as a down payment, and then borrow the rest through a mortgage. But this down payment is not your risk. Because you are responsible for the full value of the home, you are responsible for any market fluctuations. The house could lose 50% of its value, and you will still be responsible for 100% of the mortgage.

Time and fees are the other variables. Time is an integral part of real estate investing. If you buy a house, it could be decades before you realize a gain. So how will inflation hurt you? Your house will lose 3% of its value each year due to inflation, but if you have a low interest rate on your mortgage, inflation won't hurt too much. Let's say you borrowed money at a 5% interest rate, but that 5% loses 3% of value every year. So, in the end, you are only losing 2%.

Real estate is expensive and has a high barrier to entry. But performing due diligence by studying, qualifying, and quantifying all the risks, provides a good chance for a good return. Real estate, like stocks, can be a medium risk, medium reward or even a low risk, medium reward investment with the right research. Like all investments, knowing at what points you will exit the investment allows you to limit your risk.

Since medium risk/medium reward investments are the most financially efficient place to keep your money they are where you should keep most of your money.

High Risk – Variable Return:

Gambling, Lottery, Collectibles and Speculative Investments

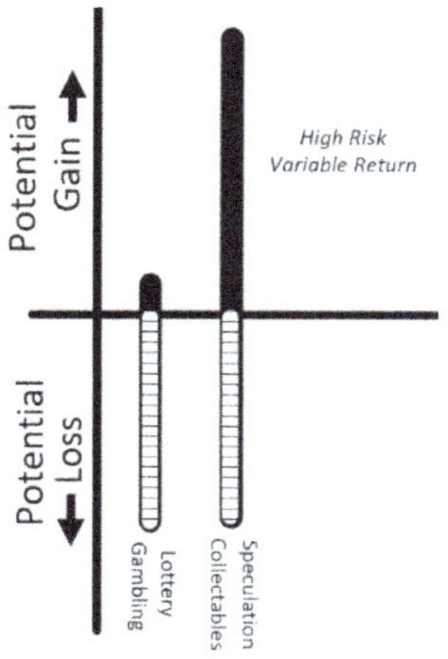

At first glance, playing the lottery or gambling seems like an easy low risk-high reward investment. Pay a dollar to win millions. But probability is important in the risk-return equation. You have a very, *very* low probability of winning and an even higher probability of losing.

And even if you *do* win, you will face high fees, taxes, and expenses. Let's say you do win the one-million-dollar lottery. If you take the lump sum, your total federal and state income taxes could be as high as 50%. Your $1M is now $500,000 (still not too bad) but you may still need to pay lawyers and accountants. If you want to be charitable (as close friends and relatives would expect) and give any significant amount of this new-found wealth away, you become liable for gift tax. Gift tax rates range from 18% to 40%, and the giver (you) pays the tax. After all is said and done, your $1M windfall could result in a $300k payout.

The result of gambling and lotteries is actually a high risk, negative reward investment. There is a potential for high reward, but this reward has a low probability. The odds are against you and out of your control. Unlike stocks or real estate, there are many risks you cannot identify or quantify. These are typically all-or-nothing investments. You are not able to put a stop-loss or low limit on the loss. The higher probability of a loss outweighs the promise of a large gain.

Investments that carry large upfront costs, fees, barriers to entry, or have 50/50 chances of making or losing money are high-risk investments because of the uncertainty of the return. There is an equal probability of negative return and positive reward.

Similarly, collectibles with small marketplaces like artwork, baseball cards, rare coins, and rare comic books are speculative investments, meaning they have a high degree of risk where prices fluctuate on factors other than pure value. These are high risk-high reward investments. As a hobby, these investments are acceptable, but your net worth should not be based on or contingent upon reaping those potential rewards.

With any high-risk purchase, investment, or activity, your intent should be to outweigh the magnitude of the opportunity cost with your happiness. You will only lose if your intent is to win financially, because big rewards require taking risks that will not pay off in the long run. If you spend money on gambling or collectibles as a means of enjoyment, that's okay; but do it in moderation and in line with your budget. But if you're seeing those expenditures as investments, you need to realize their high risk, large opportunity costs, and the significant chance of not meeting your financial milestones.

No matter what asset class you hold your money in, you should always *research the risk to realize the return.* Risk is not just volatility or 'odds', there are many factors impacting risk including probability, time and fees. You cannot eliminate the risk of any asset, but you can focus your investments in the most efficient risk-return asset classes.

How to Start Investing

Starting to invest is a big step in life. It is the realization that your future is more important than your present. If you have extra income and want to start investing in assets that appreciate but don't know where to start, it's best to talk with a financial advisor. As a general rule, you should start by building up an emergency fund and paying off any high-interest, bad loans. Once you are in a stable and financially comfortable position, start investing in pre-tax, tax-advantaged accounts. These accounts, such as your employer's 401(k), are some of the most efficient options for investing.

Once you have maxed out your pre-tax investments as allowed by the IRS, the next step is to invest in post-tax, tax-advantaged accounts, such as a Roth IRA. Although there is no tax reduction for contributions to the Roth IRA plan, qualified withdrawals from the Roth IRA plan are tax-free, as is growth in the account.

Finally, after you have reached the maximum contribution limits for all tax-advantaged accounts, the final place to invest any extra income is in regular investment accounts.

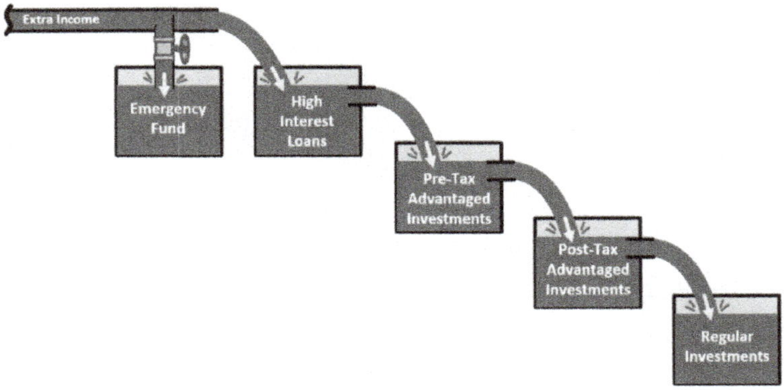

There are many online brokerages and resources for individual investors. As with all investment decisions, it is important to do your research to find the best service that meets your needs. For choosing a brokerage, I recommend looking at cost (fees), investment offerings, ease of use, and service and support.

Buying and Selling Investments

Investing is about making a present decision about future value. This simple step is burdened by risk, opportunity, bias and timing.

Consistently and reliably timing the market is impossible. "Buy low, sell high" is a cold trick some people play on the uninitiated. Of course, buy low, sell high is how you make money investing. But how do you know if the price of something is "low" or "high?"

You don't, and you can't. The trick of this rule is buried in the context. Price does not equal value. Just because something is inexpensive does not mean it has a low value. Likewise, an expensive item is not necessarily valuable.

The difference between price and value is perspective. Value is the amount of money that you are willing to pay for something. Price is the amount of money that you are asked to pay for it.

While you may not know if the *price* of an asset is low or high, you can find out if the *value* of an asset is low or high. Value investing (typically with stocks) is an investment strategy that involves buying securities that have a higher *intrinsic value* than their market price through fundamental analysis.

Market price is easy to find out by simply looking up the stock quote. Intrinsic value, however, is calculated from historical performance to find the price a rational investor is willing to pay for an investment, given its level of risk.

Intrinsic means being internal, a part of, essential, or integral to something. Intrinsic value is typically calculated by analyzing the balance sheet and financial records of a company, but everyone has a different formula. At the end of the day, intrinsic value is the price you would be willing to pay for a stock, despite its current market price.

So that's the secret to "Buy low, sell high." It is not buy at a low price, sell at a high price, it is buy low value (undervalued), hold indefinitely, and sell high value (overvalued), if at all. Yes, you only make money by selling at a higher price than you bought, but only time will tell if you bought and sold at the right time.

Some of my worst trading decisions have not been about buying stocks but *selling* stocks. I sold for no other reason than I thought the price was too high or too low. Often, I was wrong. I made the mistake of trying to time the market, of trying to get out while I thought I was ahead or had lost too much. This is the wrong mindset.

The right mindset is one of an owner for life, not a renter for an interim. You need to own like a captain, ready to ride the waves or go down with the ship. As Warren Buffet says, "The best time to buy is whenever you have money; and the best time to sell is never." Or as I like to say, "Buy whenever, hold forever, sell never."

It is not easy to never sell, but I believe it is the right plan. Unless you are forced to sell, or there is a major fundamental change to your investment, you should always hold. Consistently and reliably timing the market is impossible. Using value investing to find investments that are undervalued is a consistent way to buy quality assets. Be a collector, not a trader.

Also be aware of biases. A bias is an illogical preference, which puts disproportionate weight in favor of or against an idea. We all make judgments and have biases, so it is important to acknowledge and recognize these decisions as potentially imperfect. Biases include the idea that losses have more impact than an equivalent amount of gains (loss aversion), that information supporting existing beliefs is more accurate than the opposite (confirmation bias) and that events that occurred in the recent past will continue to occur or change unrelated future events (recency bias and gamblers fallacy).

Biases come from our unconscious mind and are obstacles to investment success. To avoid investing biases focus on removing emotions, attachment, and reactions. Instead, concentrate on your strategy and goals. Review contrary information and document your decision-making process. Ask a trusted friend or advisor. Finally, take a break and take your time. Our biases decrease over time so postponing any major decision is a good way to avoid making a wrong one.

Investing opportunity cost decisions can lead to choice overload. Investors have more choices than ever before. There are about 4,000 stocks in the U.S. markets alone. Add the number of index funds, mutual funds, bonds and real estate opportunities, and the information behind all these investments can be overwhelming. However, opportunity cost should be considered along with risk at a high level. The ultimate answer to the question of what asset classes and what investments inside the asset classes to keep your money in is up to you, your position in life and your risk tolerance.

If you need specific advice I recommend talking to a fiduciary financial advisor. In general, I recommend investing money in the most financially and risk-return efficient assets. If we redefine the risk triangle to include a mindset of a risk-return diversification built in the chapter we have this graphic:

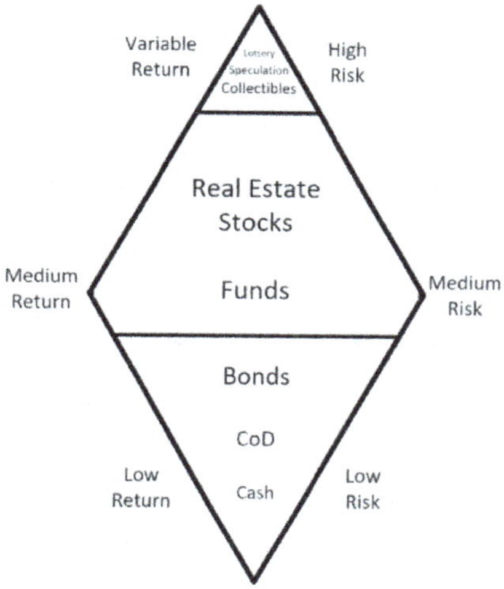

This profile is not for everyone. As we get older and closer to retirement our risk tolerance changes and so should our investment portfolios. But when we start out on our path remember, it is risker not to take risks. You know that to get to financial independence by your scheduled target, you need to invest $__,___ per year at a rate of return of _% (See page 22). The rate of return you need to achieve to reach your milestone will help you decide on where to invest. Just remember that the additional risks you take are not always equal to the potential returns.

4th Floor Summary: Invest the money saved into assets that have a greatest probability of appreciating over time. Choose assets that have favorable risk-return profiles.

The Fifth Floor: Making Money and Maximizing Your Mindset

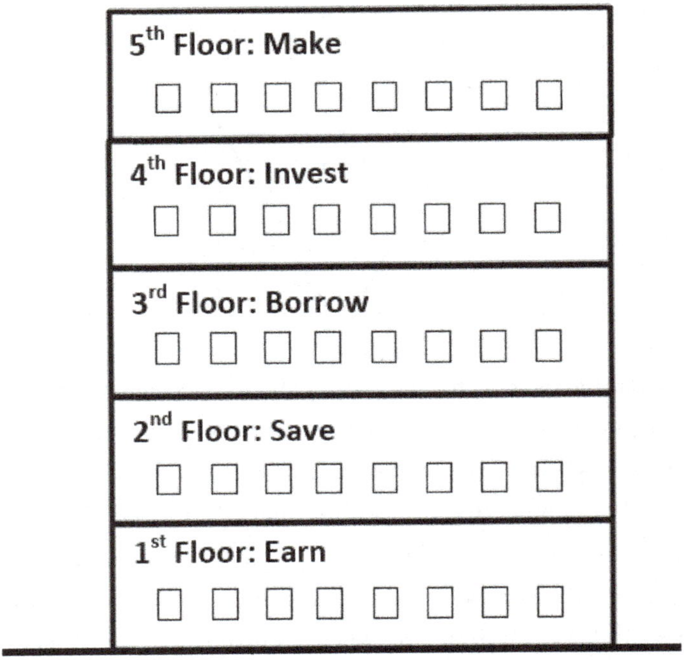

The building had been topped out; the interior work was almost done. We were testing the systems, verifying the performance, confirming the quality. We could see the finish line.

The building's future occupants were starting to scope out their new workplace. They were picking their offices, checking out their new amenities, and skeptically trying out their new open window natural ventilation system.

"What if they don't use it?" my boss asked, referring to the window system.

"That's their decision to make," I said. "We have given them the autonomy to open the windows, the control to close them, and the freedom to choose between forced, conditioned air, or natural outdoor air."

"Well, I hope they are happy, after all the work and money we put into getting the system right." My boss was right. We had spent years planning, designing, building and testing the system.

I thought back to all the time I had spent designing the system; all of the disagreements, negotiations, and compromises. It had been a long road but, in the end, we got what we envisioned—an energy saving system that will increase employee productivity. From this realization, I told my boss, "It's not about how much we spent, but how much the company will get in return."

I have heard this saying a few times from different financial professionals: "It's not about how much you earn, it's about how much you save." This is half right and half misleading. The first part is right. It's not about how much you earn from your job. But it's also not about how much you *save*. It's about how much you *make*.

Maximizing the amount of money you make shortens your path to financial independence and gives you the best chance of fulfilling the ultimate goal of maximizing your long-term happiness. The freedom, autonomy and control we've covered gets you to financial independence, but how do we maximize your money after achieving independence? Your happiness is not tied to how much money you earn, save, borrow or invest, but what you do with the money that you make.

Long-term happiness is self-sustaining. It's not about how much you earn—it's about the choices you make to keep you going. Let's take a closer look at these choices.

You make money by earning, saving, borrowing and investing. But what you really make isn't just money—it's time and opportunity—an opportunity to make decisions that affect your future time. And you have three choices: You can save money for later, spend money now, or invest money for the future.

Unfortunately, our decision-making process is mostly based on our own tacit knowledge and ability to project. The present and near future are known. The far future is unknown, and this uncertainty means you usually choose the present over the future.

Saving money can mean either keeping it to spend later or not wasting it. Saving money for later is a good choice, but is it the right choice? Remember, money by itself does not make money. Saving money does not make more opportunities. Saving money is still a short-term choice.

Spending money is trading your made money for something now. Some people with excessive outward displays of wealth make and then spend. They may spend more than they save. Sometimes, they may even spend more than they make. As discussed in the previous chapter, spending for now is for pleasure, not happiness. This instant or immediate gratification is the temptation and tendency, to forego a future benefit in order to obtain a less rewarding but more immediate benefit.

Investing is giving your money to someone else to use. Instead of retaining money, you are loaning your money out to someone else or trading your money for ownership of something. With investing, you are delegating money with the expectation that you will receive more money in the future in return. Happiness stems from our expectations. To maximize happiness we should give without the expectation of receiving.

Long-term happiness comes from what we give to receive happiness in return. The more you give, the more you receive; this is the Law of Reciprocity. You will get happiness if you help other people feel happy. Spending for now and saving for later are not giving; they are a form of taking. When you invest you are giving your money to someone else.

After making money, you have the opportunity to make these three choices. You must decide which of the three gives you the best utility. You may find utility in saving money for later or buying something you want now. But these decisions for now and later do not result in more opportunities. Consider the utility of investing to maximize your happiness.

Investing (wisely) is the only choice that gives you more opportunities. The more you invest, the more you make. The more you make, the more you create the opportunity to make more decisions. This is a compounding effect and the way to maximize happiness.

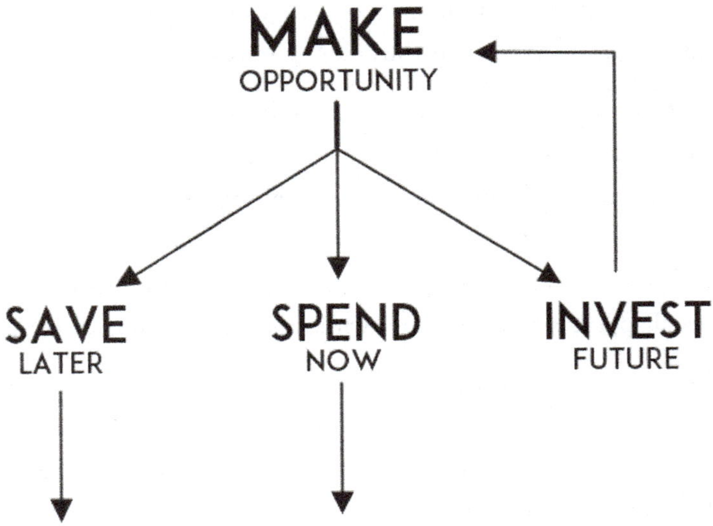

Spending now or saving for later are financial decisions that are burdened by opportunity cost. Because your investments have the potential to appreciate in value, your decisions have compounding effects in the future.

It's not about how much you earn. It's not about how much you spend. It's also not about how much you save. It's about how much you invest and make. You are not saving for retirement; you are *investing* for retirement. Your happiness, your autonomy, your ability to feel more in control is about making opportunities by investing in your future.

Having a high total net worth and reaching your milestone of financial independence is not just about *earning* money, it is about *making* money. Making money is earning plus saving, careful borrowing, investing, and holding investments in assets that appreciate in value while using active and passive income to reinvest into more appreciating assets.

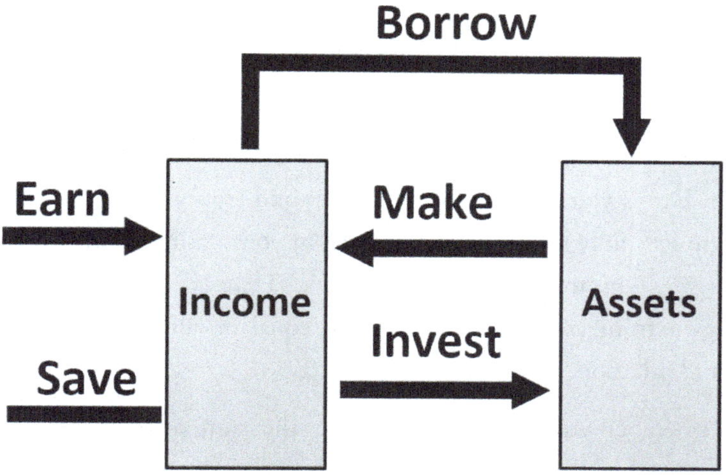

The media shows that earning money is all you need to do to become rich. The limited, traditional view is that a family can live off a single income. The head of the household will have one job from one company most of their working career and that, along with the big pension promised to him (or her, but usually the media portrays a him) upon retirement, will be sufficient to carry a whole family.

That portrayal is flawed. Working and living are much more competitive. To reach your milestone, you must earn and make money. It is not uncommon to see dual incomes in a household with both active and multiple passive income streams. If you want to reach financial independence by (or even before) your target age, it is important not only to maximize your active income but also to create multiple passive income streams.

You earn money at your job, but there is a fundamental time constraint to how much you can earn. You can only give so much time to your employers to trade for money. However, making passive income through investing separates your time from value and is a fundamental key to the right mindset. While your employer cares about how much time you put into your job, the market does not. Your assets are not valued based on the *time* you spent acquiring them, they are valued based on the *risk* you took acquiring them and while time is limited, risk is not.

When you are younger, your passive income streams will likely be smaller, but as you get close to retirement and stop working, the amount must grow to fully support your lifestyle, or your desired annual withdraw of $__,____ in today's dollars after tax. That is, the passive income flowing in from your assets alone must equal or surpass your expenses, debt, and inflation.

Remember your total net worth is the sum of your Assets Tank minus your Liabilities. Therefore, the key to increasing your total net worth is increasing your earnings, reducing your expenses, investing in assets that appreciate in value, making money, and reinvesting that money, all while limiting liabilities.

The easiest way to increase your total net worth is to set up a system of circular flow of money in your Money Flow Diagram:

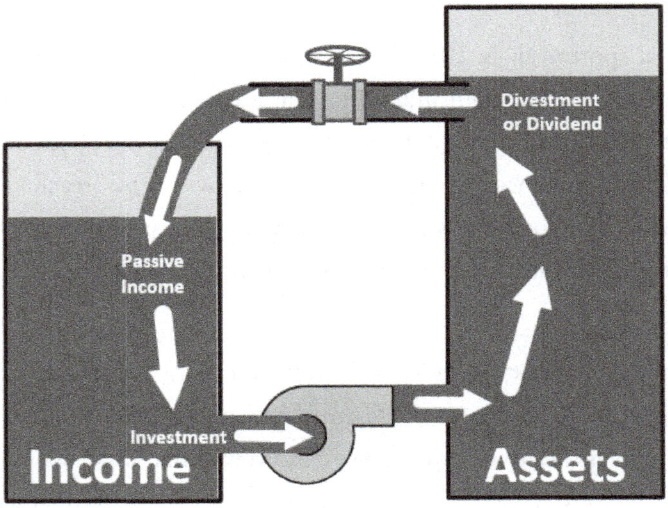

This is known as *compounding*, or the process in which an asset's profits (via capital gains, interest or dividends) are reinvested back into the existing amount to further multiply profits over time. This is the cash flow system you want to use in order to *maximize* your long-term happiness.

Albert Einstein famously said that compound interest is the most powerful force in the universe. He said, "Compound interest is the 8th wonder of the world. He who understands it, earns it; he who doesn't, pays it." Because compound interest earns interest on interest, your money multiplies at an accelerating rate.

For example, investing $10,000 today with 4% interest on average for the will results in $15,000 after 10 years, $26,700 after 25 years and $71,500 after 50 years. Visualizing this exponential growth on a graph looks like this:

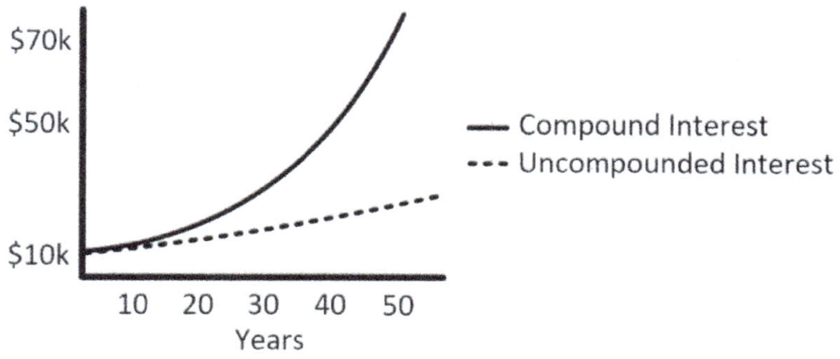

Compounding can make anyone a millionaire. The key is to start saving and investing as early as possible and stay diligent in that investment. By investing $10,000 efficiently in the stock market at an 8% return, and continuing to invest $10,000 every year, you can grow your money to $1.2M after 30 years.

Maximizing your Mindset – Happiness, Money and Time

Time is the most valuable asset you have. Recent research shows that buying time promotes happiness.[xvii] People who prioritize more free time over money report more joy in life. Financial Independence with the Right Mindset (FIRM) is having the autonomy and control to make money for the *time* to pursue your long-term happiness. Recall that the wealthy understand what the rich do not: *Money represents time and time is the goal.*

Ben Franklin may be the first person to use and understand the phrase "Time is Money." Found in his book

Time is the most valuable asset you have. Recent research shows that buying time promotes happiness.[xviii] People who prioritize more free time over money report more joy in life. Financial Independence with the Right Mindset (FIRM) is having the autonomy and control to make money for the *time* to pursue your long-term happiness. Recall that the wealthy understand what the rich do not: *Money represents time and time is the goal.*

Ben Franklin may be the first person to use and understand the phrase "Time is Money". Found in his book "*Advice to a Young Tradesman, Written by an Old One,*" the original quote is:

"Remember that Time is Money. He that can earn Ten Shillings a Day by his Labour, and goes abroad, or sits idle one half of that Day, tho' he spends but Sixpence during his Diversion or Idleness, ought not to reckon that the only Expence; he has really spent or rather thrown away Five Shillings besides."

Ben Franklin, ever the philosopher on time, also said, "You may delay, but time will not." When we think about time, we relate to it as though it is something tangible, something we can spend, save or put away for another day. We treat it as a rare commodity as we do money. However, time does not behave as a concrete substance and the more we try to contain it the less we are able to do so.[xix]

I think of time like a river you are floating down. You are not in control of your speed and you can only go one way. As you start, you have plenty of time ahead of you and all you see is a seemly endless river in front of you. But, as you age, you get closer and closer to the end of the river . . . a cliff . . . a waterfall.

Time is life's currency that you can never regain after spending it, but you can make time—free time—by making money. Making money, frees your time to pursue your purpose and find peace of mind. The pursuit of happiness is the quest for more free time to do the things you like doing.

Making money involves multiple aspects: saving, borrowing, investing, and using passive income to re-invest into more assets. Each of these steps requires making choices. You have control over these choices. Compounding the amount of money you make shortens your path to financial independence and gives you the best chance of maximizing your long-term happiness. Use what you have learned to make the right choices that lead to your milestone of financial independence and long-term happiness.

5th Floor Summary: Make your money work for you. Maximize your total net worth using compounding by reinvesting your passive income.

6. COMPLETING THE FIRM BUILDING

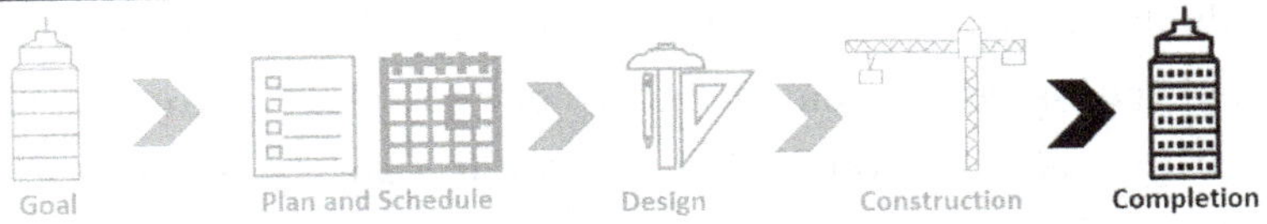

"Happiness is not in the mere possession of money; it lies in the joy of achievement, in the thrill of creative effort."
– Franklin D. Roosevelt

"I would like to congratulate everyone on your hard work. This is a premier and defining building for our company. Great job!"

It was the grand opening of the buildings and site we had worked on for years. Our upper management was giving a speech out in front of the main building.

We had overcome many adversities, but it was all worth it. There had been some casualties, but luckily, neither I nor my coworker had been fired in the process. We had been put through the wringer but came out unscathed.

Looking up at the impressive structure, I couldn't help but think of all the choices, decisions, arguments, and bruised egos that went into each aspect of the facility. Some people had already moved in, and the initial feedback was good. They liked the windows, the offices, the labs' workspaces, and the amenities. The praise and the thank you's made it all worth the effort.

Similarly, your FIRM building is complete, and I want to congratulate you. You've learned the theory and practice of creating wealth through investment. You're ready to "move in" and perform personal financial accounting by visualizing the financial flow of your money and using all five floors of your right mindset building to compound your total net worth and reach your FIRM milestone.

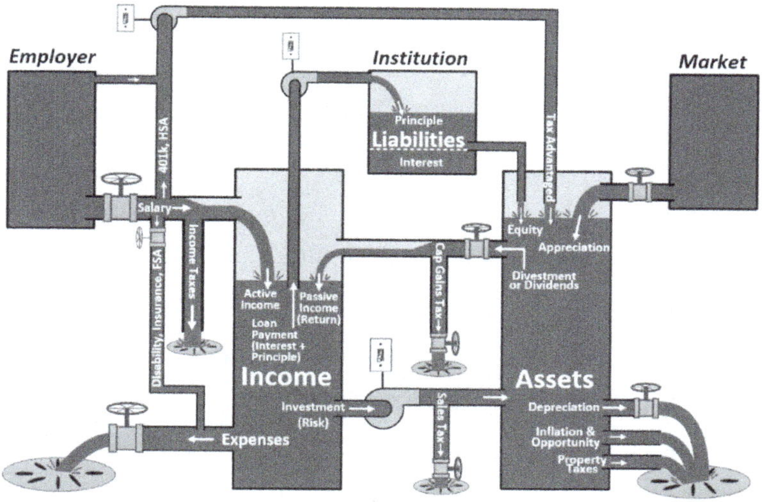

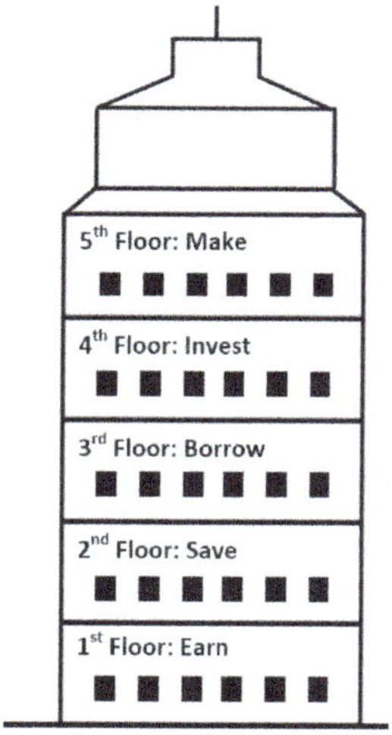

Your target total net worth of $_,___,___in future dollars was defined in the Plan and Schedule chapter and allowed your desired annual withdrawal of $___,____in today's dollars after tax and after paying any debts. To get to this financially independent total net worth by the target date, your plan is to invest $___,____per year at a rate of return of _%.

To execute your plan and get to that amount, you built these mindset floors and will make the right choices at each floor:

1st Floor: Start with your salary. Earn as much as possible to provide adequate active income. Evaluate your future job prospects. Negotiate whenever possible.

2nd Floor: Save as much as you can by reducing expenses, taxes, and exposure to inflation. Only spend on expenses that contribute to long-term happiness.

3rd Floor: Borrow as needed, but only when the rate of interest is less than what you would lose to inflation. Liabilities are responsibilities, so choose wisely when taking on debt.

4th Floor: Invest the money saved into assets that have a greater probability of appreciating over time. Choose assets that have favorable risk-return profiles.

5th Floor: Make your money work for you. Maximize your total net worth utilizing compounding by reinvesting your passive income.

7. LIVING IN THE FIRM BUILDING

"Achievement of your happiness
is the only moral purpose of your life."
– Ayn Rand

I started this book with a review of the timeless story of *The Giving Tree* about a tree, a boy, and the focus of happiness. What made the tree happy was sharing time with the boy and using her time to help make him happy (her purpose). As the boy grew up, he had to leave the tree to pursue his own path towards happiness. The tree was happy to help, but sad because of the separation. But, in the end, the boy returned, giving the tree both the shared time and ability to help which makes her happy by fulfilling her purpose.

Too many people believe that all they need to do to be happy is to become rich by winning the lottery or inheriting a million dollars so they can retire without worrying about finances. Unfortunately, without a plan, purpose, autonomy or control of the movement of money in your financial tanks, money can flow out just as easily as it can flow in. Because the flow of money and wealth are difficult to visualize, I created the financial flow system diagram in this book to help you understand this critical process.

We started with a FIRM framework:

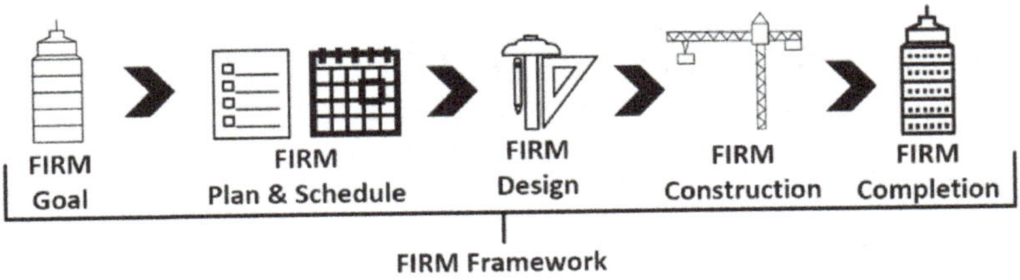

This framework represents the sum of your experience, knowledge, and understanding from this book. We defined a goal, created a plan, designed our understanding, constructed our knowledge and completed our building. The framework interlinked items that support the right approach to your specific objective and it serves as a guide to your destination. By using the FIRM framework, you have built your FIRM building.

You know how to make the right choices to put yourself on your path to long-term happiness. Understand your goal, plan and schedule around that goal, design a system to visualize your plan, and execute the plan to reach your milestone using your right mindset.

The future seems scary. The problem of planning for the future is compounded by the paralyzing fear of making a wrong move because there's so much to lose. War, climate change, market crashes, market bubbles, meteors, etc. There is a reason why doomsayers are much more popular than people who say the future will just be fine. Fear of the future is fear of forward movement in the face of the unknown. But think about it this way: you've made it this far and you are okay, so why shouldn't the future be brighter? There are many things out of our control, so don't worry about trying to control them. What you can control are your decisions—including your decision to plan and to stick to your plan.

Even harder than planning is executing on a long-term plan. To reach our goal we need to stop thinking about short-term benefits and enjoyment and start making decisions that may require struggle now but pay off big later. Every day we will face challenges and exceptions that go against our plan. If we think something should be easy and it turns out to be hard, we get upset and are more likely to give up. Changing our behaviors means having the willpower to overcome these challenges.

Challenge yourself to reach your milestone of financial independence with the right mindset by using your autonomy and control to maximize the money you make. *Make* money by earning plus saving, borrowing, and investing. When you are in a position of sufficient worth from *making* money to live your desired lifestyle you won't have to depend on *earning* income from employment and your future will be wide open. You will have the free time to pursue your purpose and find peace of mind. You will go from saying, "There is so much I *have* to do!" to "There is so much I *can* do!"

The pursuit of long-term happiness is about your journey through life on the route of your choosing, not the destination. All successful journeys require two things which you have now; autonomy and control. You are equipped with the knowledge to make informed, independent choices and the control to stick with them. Reaching financial independence ensures your freedom to pursue your self-sustaining happiness. Maximizing (compounding) the amount of money you make shortens your path to financial independence and gives you the best chance of maximizing your long-term happiness. Money can buy happiness, if you have the right mindset.

My hope is that, like *The Giving Tree*, I have given you the necessary wisdom and tools to make more of what you want. I wish you well on your journey of ***Building FIRM*** and long-term happiness.

LONG TERM
HAPPINESS
FINANCIAL
INDEPENDENCE
PATHS OF OPPORTUNITY

END NOTES

[i] Silverstein, Shel. The Giving Tree. New York, Ny, Harpercollins Publishers, 2014.

[ii] Kehoe, Meg. "The One Thing You Never Knew About 'The Giving Tree.'" Romper, 2016, www.romper.com/p/the-one-thing-you-never-knew-about-the-giving-tree-10280.

[iii] Cherry, Kendra. "What Is Learned Helplessness and Why Does It Happen?" Verywell Mind, Verywellmind, 4 June 2009, www.verywellmind.com/what-is-learned-helplessness-2795326.

[iv] Deci, Edward & Ryan, Richard. (2008). Hedonia, Eudaimonia, and Well-Being: an Introduction. Journal of Happiness Studies. 9. 1-11. 10.1007/s10902-006-9018-1.

[v] The 2020 World Happiness Report reviews data from thousands of people around the world. Six factors are used to explain happiness, and four of these measure different aspects of the social environment: having someone to count on, having a sense of freedom to make key life decisions, generosity, and trust. T Helliwell, John F., Richard Layard,Jeffrey Sachs, and Jan-Emmanuel De Neve, eds. 2020.World Happiness Report 2020. New York: Sustainable Development Solutions Network.

[vi] Frankl, Viktor E, et al. Man's Search for Meaning. Boston, Beacon Press, 2017.

[vii] Jefferson, Thomas. Declaration of Independence. 1776.

[viii] Locke, John. An Essay Concerning Human Understanding. Volume II. United States, Createspace Independent Publishing Platform, 2014.

[ix] Earl Carter 1980; "America's Army", Beth Bailey, Pages 191, 192.

[x] Robin, Vicki, et al. Your Money or Your Life : 9 Steps to Transforming Your Relationship with Money and Achieving Financial Independence. New York, Penguin Books, 2008.

[xi] Adamczyk, Alicia. "Here's How to Figure out How Much Money You Need to Retire Early." CNBC, 27 June 2019, www.cnbc.com/2019/06/27/how-to-figure-out-how-much-money-you-need-to-retire-early.html. Accessed 26 July 2020.

[xii] Parsons, Rob. Heart of Success : Making It in Business without Losing in Life. Hodder & Stoughton Ltd, 2009.

[xiii] Bronnie Ware. The Top Five Regrets of the Dying : A Life Transformed by the Dearly Departing. Alexandria, Nsw, Hay House Australia, 2019.

[xiv] McMahon, Tim. "US Inflation Long Term Average." Inflationdata.Com, Apr. 2014, inflationdata.com/Inflation/Inflation_Rate/Long_Term_Inflation.asp.

[xv] Frankel, Matthew. "What's the Average American's Tax Rate?" The Motley Fool, The Motley Fool, 4 Mar. 2017, www.fool.com/retirement/2017/03/04/whats-the-average-americans-tax-rate.aspx. Accessed 15 Mar. 2019.

[xvi] Inc, iA. "Money, Quality and Time." Medium, 17 Jan. 2018, medium.com/@ia/money-quality-and-time-2914cbe4636e#:~:text=Saving%20money%20short%20term%20can%20waste%20time%20long%20term. Accessed 8 Aug. 2020.

[xvii] Whillans, Ashley V., et al. "Buying Time Promotes Happiness." Proceedings of the National Academy of Sciences, vol. 114, no. 32, 24 July 2017, pp. 8523–8527, 10.1073/pnas.1706541114.

[xviii] Whillans, Ashley V., et al. "Buying Time Promotes Happiness." Proceedings of the National Academy of Sciences, vol. 114, no. 32, 24 July 2017, pp. 8523–8527, 10.1073/pnas.1706541114.

[xix] Shir-Wise, Michelle. Time, Freedom and the Self: The Cultural Construction of "free" Time. Cham, Switzerland, Palgrave Macmillan, 2019.

Made in the USA
Monee, IL
04 November 2026

67386432R00089